Crimes Against The Heart

Escaping The Prison of Darkness Into God's Marvellous Light

By

Rose Robinson Coleman

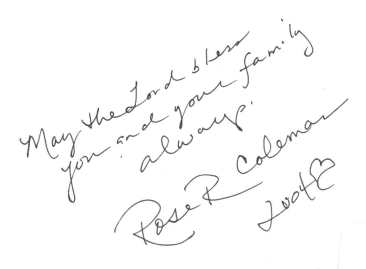

May the Lord bless you and your family always.
Rose R Coleman 2008

ISBN: 1-4140-1964-5 (e-book)
ISBN: 1-4140-1963-7 (Paperback)
ISBN: 1-4140-1962-9 (Dust Jacket)

This book is printed on acid free paper.

Scriptures from the King James version of The Bible

1stBooks — rev. 10/27/03

Content

Acknowledgements
Free At Last

Anger 1
Attitude 14
Bitterness 27
Bondage In Sin 37
Depression 47
Disappointment 58
Discouraged 70
Fear 81
Guilt 94
Hatred 106
Insecurity 117
Loneliness 126
Rejection 142
Sickness 157
Sorrow 172
Stress 199
Temptation 212
Unforgiveness 219
Unwilling To Change 229
Worry 234

Acknowledgments

To my family and friends in Christ Jesus

I am more than a conqueror

because you cared for me in a special way

I am more than a conqueror

because your love and support never fades

In every battle, I have been tested

But through faith I will survive

Thank you for showing me that

I am a more than a conqueror

Through our Lord and Saviour

Jesus Christ.

"These trials are only to test your faith, to show that it is strong and pure. It is being tested as fire tests and purifies gold — and your faith is far more precious to God than mere gold. So if your faith remains strong after being tried by fiery trials, it will bring you much praise and glory and honor on the day when Jesus Christ is revealed to the whole world."
1 Peter 1:7

Free At Last

I know the chains that had me bound
One by one they tried to consume me
The guilt of letting you down
Tried to ruin me, it tried to kill me
The chains of depression had a gripe on my mind
The chains of rejection would not let me go
The chains of fear kept me discouraged at times
The chains of unforgiveness kept me alone
The chains of hatred had a lock on my heart
The chains of insecurity had me questioning myself
The chains of disappointment kept hitting like a fiery dart
The chains of bitterness made me feel less and less
The chains of sickness robbed me of many years
The chains of anger destroyed many relationships
The chains of sorrow just left me in bitter tears
The chains of temptation destroyed many friendships
The chains of worry kept weighing me down
The bondage of sin negatively affected my attitude
The chains of stress turned my smile into a frown
Oh Lord, Oh Lord, what must I do?

Dear, these trials are only a test of your faith
A test to show that you can be strong and endure
Your faith is far more precious than gold
More precious than silver so pure
These chains keep you in the deepest pit
Keeps you in the miry clay
It keeps you from escaping the prison of darkness
Into the glorious light of day
I am the God of Abraham
I am Jehovah
I am your Help
I am your Comforter
I am the Prince of Peace
I am King of Kings

I am Jesus Christ
I am your Saviour
If you call on me anytime, anywhere
You will win every battle, pass every test
Instead of darkness you will see
God's marvelous light and glory
Then you will know
you are free at last.

"I will freely sacrifice unto thee: I will praise thy name, O LORD; for it is good. For he hath delivered me out of all trouble: and mine eye hath seen his desire upon mine enemies."
Psalm 54:6-7

Anger

Psalm 90:7-8
[7]For we are consumed by thine anger, and by thy wrath are we troubled.
[8]Thou hast set our iniquities before thee, our secret sins in the light of thy countenance.

Anger Management Prayer

Frustration has got a hold of me today
Lord, what am I to do
I have a list of ugly things I want to say
But I know they will surely offend you.
I am angry at the world it seems
There is nothing going my way
I am pressured, upset, and mad you see
Which is why I am trying to pray.
Lord, I know I should not let my problems
Get the best of me today
But I am tired and weak; it is help that I seek
Problems keep mounting up to my dismay.
I am mad at my husband; the kids are getting on my nerves
And there are overdue bills that need to be paid
My dinner is burning, my mind is just yearning
To start yelling and screaming but instead I must pray.

So, dear Lord, here I am ready to explode
Give me your guidance to correct my emotions
I am like a wayward ship tossed to and fro
In a raging storm in the middle of the ocean.
"My child, my child, do you not understand
That I can help you conquer everything
What you must do is take a hold of my hand
Allow me to guide you each and every day.
For I am your God who created the heavens
There is nothing I cannot do
But you must give me your burdens; you must give me your pain
Put me first in your life; Not everything is about you.
Do not let frustrations pull you further away
From the path that I have set for you
You must always keep your heart and mind clear
When I send my Holy Spirit to comfort you.
Do not let anger paralyze you
To the point that it separates you

From those who love you and from those who care
Despite all of your problems and misfortunes
You must keep the faith; all it takes is a prayer."

O, dear Lord, I have failed at this test
To respond in a Christian way
Please forgive me, dear Lord
Help me to think clearly dear Lord
In all that I do; help me to remember to pray.
In Jesus name,
Amen.

"Cease from anger, and forsake wrath: fret not thyself in any wise to
do evil."
Psalm 37:8

Love Bonds Us Together

What can separate us from the love of God?
Hatred, jealousy, malice, and shame
For these things fuel the fire of destruction
So we must be diligent to extinguish the flame.

For we are all God's beautiful children
No matter the color, the status, or the name
For there is no difference between us
When we stand before Him, we are the same.

We must treat each other with humility
We must treat each other with respect and grace
We must love one another always
Regardless of our religion or race.

For we are a chosen people
Dearly loved by the Father above
Because if God can love us unconditionally
Then we must live by his example of love.

Great is the love God bestows upon us
To cleanse us from all of our sins
When Christ died on the cross, He saved us
From the iniquities of the world we live in.

So be filled with compassion for the lonely
Be gentle and kind when you encounter mistakes
Show mercy for the meek and downtrodden
No matter the situation, always keep the faith.

For our mission is very simple
It has always been a part of God's plan
To just live your life fully for the Lord
And always love your fellow man.

If God's spirit does not shine in your heart
Then the light of love cannot manifest itself
You must pray for those who persecute you
And love your neighbor as you love yourself.

So stand firm on the foundation of God's promises
When trials and tribulations come your way
For divided we are weak; united we are strong
His love bonds us together always.

"Beloved, let us love one another: for love is of God; and every one
that loveth is born of God, and knoweth God. He that loveth not
knoweth not God for God is love."
I John 4:7-8

Do Unto The Least Of These

Do you see what you do at home
is for the glory of God?
Do you complain about keeping the house in order
or do you do all things in love?
As you wash and scrub
As you cook and clean
Do you praise the Lord
or do you just scream?
If your children are bad
And everything makes you mad
Do you curse and holler
or does your heart sing?
Often times we feel unappreciated
Often times we feel just worn out
Often times we are taken for granted
But how do you think God feels
When we respond wrong and just pout?
In everything we must do it in love
Even when things are pressing us
In everything we must have patience
Even when things are causing a fuss
Your children are a gift from God
No matter what you are to take care of them
Your husband is the head of the household
Do whatever it takes to take care of him
You, my lady, may feel lost in the shuffle
But do not fret for your help comes from within
Just remember
whatever you do unto the least of these brothers of mine
You did for Jesus Christ, your Savior and friend.

"I tell you the truth, whatever you did for one of the least of these
brothers of mine, you did for me."
Matthew 25:40

Praying for Rain

Oh Lord, most gracious God
Who is clothed in honour and majesty
Who laid the foundation of the earth
Who healeth all sickness; who forgives my iniquities.

Rain your holy anointing down upon me I pray
For I need a cleansing right now
My spirit is in a dark place this very moment
Every aspect of my life is turned upside down.

Clean my heart, Lord, remove all that hinders me
Clear my mind, Lord, please remove those things
That keeps me from getting close to you
Remove the obstacles and all the pain that they bring.

Remove that prideful spirit that keeps me bitter
Remove all envy, all anger, and all strife
Rain your holy anointing down upon me right now
Cleanse me O Lord; remove the misery from my life.

Show me thy mercy O Lord; grant me thy forgiveness
Give ear unto my prayer dear Lord, show me your grace
Redeem my soul and give me strength to survive
Deliver me from this bondage; restore me to thy holy place.

For you are God Almighty, You are most holy
There is no other name above your glorious name
You created the heavens in its marvellous splendor
You are Omnipotent; you are worthy of all my praise.

I lay my life before you most gracious God
Blessings and honour, glory and power to you always
Save me O Lord; open the floodgates of heaven upon me

7

Rain down your Holy anointing; shower me with your love
In the matchless name of Jesus Christ, I pray.
Amen.

"Having therefore these promises, dearly beloved, let us cleanse
ourselves from all filthiness of the flesh and spirit, perfecting holiness
in the fear of God."
II Corinthians 7:1

"You heavens above, rain down righteousness; let the clouds shower
it down. Let the earth open wide, let salvation spring up, let
righteousness grow with it; I, the LORD, have created it."
Isaiah 45:8

Teach Me O God

Search me O God and know my heart
Teach me to do thy will
Show thy ways and the path I must take
Teach me dear Lord to stand still.

Try me O God and know my thoughts
Teach me to quietly listen for you
for your Word is sweet fragrance that awakens me
Refresh me O Lord like the morning's dew.

Chastise me O God and cleanse my soul
Teach me thy patience and grace
Show me thy love; keep me I pray
Restore me for thy righteous sake.

Bless me O God and know my deeds
Teach me to lift up my eyes towards you
for you are my help; in you will I trust
Only in you Lord will I be renewed.

As I glorify thee, O God, hear my praise
As I pray Lord hear my plea
I will be still until your will is done
I am a willing vessel
O God Almighty,
teach me, teach me.

"Cause me to hear thy loving kindness in the morning; for in thee do
I trust: cause me to know the way wherein I should walk; for I lift up
my soul unto thee... Teach me thy will; for thou art my God: thy
spirit is good: lead me into the land of uprightness."
Psalm 143:8,10

Humble Pie

To be filled by His Holy Spirit
To do God's will
To be in His divine presence
I am not worthy of any of this.

To live my life cleanly
To be honorable and loved
To be a Christian example
I find it hard to keep up.

To not smolder with anger
To pray through problems that I face
To strive to just be happy
I must be diligent to win this race.

To have patience to wait
To survive through every test
To be filled with compassion
I must take control of my stress.

To chastise the flesh and conquer sin
To overcome all of the pain
To become a better person
I must let go of the shame.

To not be discouraged
To not let others pull me away
To instead walk in faith
I know I must now pray.

To submit myself therefore to God
To humble myself in the sight of His Holiness
To repent for my shortcomings
I bow down and ask for His forgiveness.

To chastise this earthly vessel
To have the strength to take a stand
To be victorious, Lord please forgive me...
I am only human.

"But we have this treasure in earthen vessels, that the excellency of
the power may be of God, and not of us. We are troubled on every
side, yet not distressed: we are perplexed, but not in despair:
Persecuted, but not forsaken: cast down, but not destroyed: Always
bearing about in the body the dying of the Lord Jesus, that the life
also of Jesus, that the life also of Jesus might be made manifest in our
body."
II Corinthians 4:7-9

Song Of Praise

O Lord, thy Lord, you are my strength
O Lord, thy Lord, you are my song
Lord, you're my salvation
that I draw joyfully from
Oh Lord, I praise your Holy name.

Although Lord you were angry
at all of the times I failed
Your anger has turned away from me
Once I started drawing from your well
I can call on your name
I will trust and be not afraid
Oh Lord, I give you all the praise.

Lord I give thanks
for your glorious salvation
Lord, I give thanks
for all the marvellous things you have done
I will shout Hallelujah
I will sing for joy
I will exalt your great name all over the world.

O Lord, thy Lord, you are my strength
O Lord, thy Lord, you are my song
Lord, you're my salvation
that I draw joyfully from
Oh Lord, I praise your Holy name
You are Jesus Christ
Oh, Lord, I praise your Holy name
You are God
Oh, Lord, I praise your Holy name.

"And in that day thou shalt say, O LORD, I will praise thee: though thou wast angry with me, thine anger is turned away, and thou comfortedst me. Behold, God is my salvation; I will trust, and not be afraid: for the LORD JEHOVAH is my strength and my song; he also is become my salvation. Therefore with joy shall ye draw water out of the wells of salvation. And in that day shall ye say, Praise the LORD, call upon his name, declare his doings among the people, make mention that his name is exalted. Sing unto the LORD; for he hath done excellent things: this is known in all the earth. Cry out and shout, thou inhabitant of Zion: for great is the Holy One of Israel in the midst of thee."

Isaiah 12:1-6

Attitude

Luke 12:2-3
[2]For there is nothing covered, that shall not be revealed; neither hid, that shall not be known. [3]Therefore whatsoever ye have spoken in darkness shall be heard in the light; and that which ye have spoken in the ear in closets shall be proclaimed upon the housetops.

Keep Your Lamp Shining

When trials and tribulations come your way
And burdens fall upon you like rain
You have to keep your lamp shining
You have to shelter it from the pain
You have to fill it with anointing oil
That comes from praying in Jesus name.

When your fuse seems a little short
And your lamp is in need of a fix
Dive into God's Word and He will reveal a plan
That will brighten up your life
It will strengthen you again
Place your lamp on God's Word
For on a solid foundation will it stand
Do all that you do for God and not for man
Then your fuse will grow tall and strong again.

You got to keep your lamp shining
Do not lose your glow for one day
For when the hour does come
It will brighten the way
You do not want to be left behind
Because when Jesus does returns
You will not know the day or the time
Make sure your flame always burns.

So be on fire for the Lord
Despite what the devil brings
Do not get discouraged nor give in to anything
You got to keep your lamp shining
Through the pain and the rain
Keep your lamp shining
Make sure yours is an everlasting flame.
Remove any obstacles
So that others will see your light

So that those who are lost
Can be guided to Jesus Christ
The lamp of the Lord is searching
Your spirit for its flame
It searches out from your inmost being
To see what has been done in Jesus name.

So let your light shine
Fuel it with the Word of God
Keep your lamp ready
Shined and polished, cleansed and scrubbed
But most of all be ready
To give an account for your flame
Fill your lamp with the fruit of the spirit
And let it be a witness in Jesus name

Then your lamp will be placed
In the right hand of God
When your chariot come to pick it up for it heavenly ride
He will take one look at its beauty
And then with love He will say
"Well Done" .

"For You will light my lamp; The Lord my God will enlighten my
darkness."
Psalm 18:29

"Those who are wise shall shine like the brightness of the firmament,
and those who turn many to righteousness like the stars forever and
ever."
Daniel 12:3

The Pressures Of Life

Pulling, tugging, stretching, mashing
Bending, kneading, pushing, lashing
Dragging, conforming, smashing, deforming
Scorching, burning, melting, yearning
Going, going, going, gone
That is what happens when things go wrong
When the pressures of this world try to attack
Know that God will protect you and start fighting back
Use gentleness, meekness, temperance, and patience
Hopefulness, faithfulness, kindness, and goodness
Loving, caring, be joyful and at peace
Believing, receiving, sharing, and just cease
Rising, rising, rising, above
That is what happens when you abide in God's love.

"But the fruit of the Spirit is love, joy, peace, longsuffering, kindness, goodness, faithfulness, gentleness, self-control. Against such there is no law."
Galatians 5:22-23

"These six things the LORD hates, Yes, seven are an abomination to Him:
A proud look,
A lying tongue,
Hands that shed innocent blood,
A heart that devises wicked plans,
Feet that are swift in running to evil,
A false witness who speaks lies,
And one who sows discord among brethren."
Proverbs 6:17-18

Watch What You Say

If you are trying to live a Christian life
Harboring resentment will lead you astray
So before you allow yourself to react
Take heed of what you will say.

When your spouse does things to upset you
And your child's behavior makes you ashamed
Remember the Word of the Lord
Before you use His name in vain.

The tongue can be sharp like a knife
It can cut deep into the mind and heart
So before you pierce someone with your words
Bind your tongue; keep it sweet, not tart.

Give gentle answers when wrath approaches
For a harsh word will make matters bad
Let knowledge command what you will say
Do not be foolish; keep your heart glad.

For a wise person's heart guides his mouth
And his lips bring instructions to grow
But a foolish person's lips can bring him strife
And hurt everyone he knows.

So allow the spirit to dwell within you
Fill your mind with the goodness you seek
Then only kindness, meekness, and pure thoughts
Will be evident when you speak.

So listen first, then gather your thoughts
Let your words reflect the Lord today
Because no matter what the situation is
Think first and watch what you say.

"Be not rash with thy mouth, and let not thine heart be hasty to utter any thing before God: for God is in heaven, and thou upon earth: therefore let thy words be few."
Ecclesiastes 5:2

"The heart of the wise teacheth his mouth, and addeth learning to his lips. Pleasant words are as an honeycomb, sweet to the soul, and health to the bones."
Proverbs 16:23-24

Learn To Love Your Job

It is time to make peace
With the job that you have
Even when times are hard
And everything makes you mad.

If this job that you work
Is strangling the life out of you
Then it is time for a change
And here is what you must do.

You must take the Lord with you
When you enter the building
You must pray for guidance
When that project is winning.

You must ask Him for strength
When things get out of hand
You must ask Him for patience
When there is too much demand.

This job can help you blossom
Like a flower in springtime
Or you can let it destroy you
By letting it mess with your mind.

Do not let the devil steal
Another moment from your life
By being angry, hurt, or frustrated
Do not let it cause you more strife.

Let your job bring out the best in you
Let your dreams become your career
Just ask the Lord to bless you
Do it for Him and do it well.

Always be a Christian example
When handling stress at the workplace
Believe in yourself, your wisdom, and know
Those things will run with the Lord's grace.

So learn to love your job today
And you will begin to find
That the Lord can definitely change it
And bless you with a better one next time.

"And whatsoever ye do, do it heartily, as to the Lord, and not unto men; Knowing that of the Lord ye shall receive the reward of the inheritance: for ye serve the Lord Christ."
Colossians 3:23-24

A Prayer of Thanksgiving

As I enter into this prayer, I know I am truly blessed
For my days have been bountiful and my nights have been just rest
Before I start a brand new day, I want to lift my hands to thee
To praise you and to give you thanks for all you have done for me.

Lord, I thank you for my health and for keeping me so well
Lord, I thank you for my family and for the life you gave me here
Where would I be without your love, I do not ever want to know
There's no doubt that I would be lost… thanks for saving my soul.

I thank you for your son, Jesus, who died on Calvary
To save a poor, wretched, sinful soul just like me
I thank you for your peace and for your ever-saving grace
You love me unconditionally and I know I will win this race.

Lord, I thank you for my home and for the things to me you gave
Lord, I thank you for my job and for the stress that comes my way
For I know with all the dark clouds, perseverance is my goal
It may be a storm, but with your help onward I will go.

I thank you for the sunshine when things are looking gloom
For the overflow of blessings…in my cup there's no more room
Lord, I thank you for your patience and for waiting to see
That I will put my trust in you and know that prayer is the key.

Lord, I thank you for my friends and for the life you gave to me
Lord, I thank you for the moon, the stars, for food to not go hungry
Where would I be without your strength, I do not ever want to know
You are such an awesome God and that is why I praise you Lord.

As I end this prayer of thanks, I will give you all the praise
I will give you the glory; with my voice, your name I will raise
Where you will be is in my heart, for the price for me was paid
Thanks for being merciful, Lord, I will love you always.

Where you will be is in my mind; a brand new life I have found
Where you will be is in my soul so I can be heaven bound
I thank you now and forever for being my Saviour, my friend
In Jesus glorious and wonderful name I thank you, Amen.

"Giving thanks always for all things unto God and the Father in the
name of our Lord Jesus Christ"
Ephesians 5:20

Dance Before The Lord

I close my eyes as I prepare my spirit to dance
For I want to give reverence to my Lord, my God
As I gather my being I begin to shake
The cares of this world begin to fall
The stress of my day
The frustrations, the anxieties, the weight
All fell off of my spirit
I begin to feel lighter
For my burdens were released
I am now ready to dance before the Lord.

I step into his holy presence
I bow down before my Lord
For He is Holy
All majesty and honor surrounds him
All glory and all power belongs to him
I knew in my heart that I must dance
For my Lord is worthy to be praised
But I must come with a humble spirit
One that will worship God in spirit and in truth
And for that I did not feel worthy to be before him.

I must come before God a willing vessel
A living testimony of all that He had done for me
Not in body nor in mind but in spirit
And at that very point I began to flow
I lifted up my hands in thanksgiving to my Lord
As I sashayed into his courts with praise
I twirled around in honor of him
As I mentioned his Holy Name
Jesus, my Saviour
Almighty God
My Deliverer, my Comforter
My Lord
I danced.

I began to sing a heavenly melody in my heart
As I danced from east to west
The harp of my soul begin to play
As I swayed from north to south
Hands clapping, feet stomping
I sent praises up gloriously to my Lord
Hallelujah to my King
To show him how thankful I am for my life
To worship, to adore the very essence
Of my Lord and Saviour, Jesus
I praised his holy name.

Then my spirit began to settle itself
As I slowed down to a solemn pace
I bowed before him once again
To worship and to seek his face
Tears came streaming down my eyes
As my life begin to erase
I looked up to see such a glorious sight
As his heavenly light shined down upon me
Draped by his love and his Holy Spirit Divine
My Lord lifted me up and He saved me
In my spirit I knew that He was well pleased
At the offering that I gave
And with the next breath I deeply inhaled
And then my arms begin to wave
Side to side, up and down
Into a cross they positioned themselves
Then wrapping each arm around me
The warmth of God love was surely felt.

He reminded me that the ultimate sacrifice
Was made at Calvary
When He died on the cross to save a soul
That looked just like me
He then lifted my face to look to the hills
To which cometh all of my help

He then filled me with his Holy Spirit
I had worship the Lord in the beauty of his holiness
As I bowed down before him again.

Then I departed from his holy presence
But I knew I was not alone
For the Lord showed me how to be strong
I felt renewed and rejuvenated
I felt purged; I felt cleansed
I felt loved beyond all measure
From that day on as I entered into my prayer closet
As I bowed down before him
As I enter into his holy presence forevermore
I will praise my Saviour; I will worship Him
In spirit and in truth
When I dance before the Lord.

"Know the Lord, he is God; It is He who has made us, and not we
ourselves;
We are His people and the sheep of His pasture. Enter into His gates
with thanksgiving, and into his courts with praise. Be thankful to
Him, and bless His name. For the Lord is good;
His mercy is everlasting, and His truth endures to all generations."
Psalm 100:3-5

"Give to the Lord the glory due His name; Bring an offering, and
come before Him.
Oh, worship the Lord in the beauty of holiness."
1 Chronicles 16:29

Bitterness

Job 3:19-20

[19]The small and great are there; and the servant is free from his master.

[20]Wherefore is light given to him that is in misery, and life unto the bitter in soul;

Let It Go

"Into Your hands I commit My spirit"
was the last thing that Jesus said
As He died upon the cross at Calvary
Having said this, He breathed His last
For all that He had endured
All the hurt, humiliation, and pain
Jesus released from himself all the love he had
And save us from our sins.

If Jesus can let go of all the wrongs
That was done to him upon the cross
Why should we keep holding on to hurt and pain
If his life paid the cost?

Why do we keep holding onto pride?
Why do we get angry or even sad?
Why do we doubt and why do we lie?
Why do we spend so much energy getting mad?
Why can't we forgive and forget
Just like our Savoir did for us?
Why do we have to be selfish or even vain?
Why do we get sick and just give up?

It is time to let go of the emotions
That keeps dragging you down
It is time to say farewell to the problems
That keeps hanging around
It is time to let go and let God
Take control of your life situations
It is time to give to him your burdens
He will provide however long the duration.

Let go of the hurt and replace it with forgiveness
Let go of the pride and the shame
Let go of all the confusion in your life

It is time to heal; let go of the pain.
The world is driven by emotions
And the devil wants to take you for a ride
For it were the emotions of a confused people
That allowed Jesus to be crucified.

So put yourself at Calvary
Say it is finished, let those emotions die
Commit your spirit into the hands of your Father
Let it go and let God.

"And when Jesus had cried with a loud voice, he said, Father, into thy hands I commend my spirit: and having said thus, he gave up the ghost."

Luke 23:46

Blue River

Flowing down quietly, without fear
The bittersweet essences of my tears
Down into the valley in pain they call
Downward like a waterfall.

The pit of my being begins to fill
As my heart bleeds with sorrowful tears
What was once so shiny and bright
Has now given way to the darkest of night.

The sparkle that was once in my eyes
No longer flickers for the flame has now died
So I close them for there are no more tears to cry
And then I ask the Lord why, oh why?

Before me I see my river so blue
So deep with suffering it is full
It flows from the direction of my heart
Which has a wound the size of a dart.

The enemy came to cause harm
And he caught me unarmed
No shield of faith, not even my sword
Which is God's Holy Word.

My river flows into God's right hand
Its deepest blue makes me weep again
But this time it is for joy
Because I know now where my river flows.

Even though I was caught unprepared
God never gives me more than I can bear
He touched my sorrowful river so blue
Replaced it with peace and gave me life anew.

I am reminded that it takes God's Word
To overcome the iniquities of this sinful world
With thanksgiving I send praises up above
My clear river now reflects God's rainbow of love.

"Though I walk in the midst of trouble, thou wilt revive me: thou
shalt stretch forth thine hand against the wrath of mine enemies, and
thy right hand shall save me."
Psalm 138:7

Bittersweet

Bitter...

Gives way to negativity that drains you like a scorching desert
It will sap every drop of love until the well runs dry
It will devour you like a deadly virus
It will leave a hurtful, painful wound inside.

Bitterness can transform you into an ungrateful soul
It will rob you of all joy and happiness
It will send you on a long, perilous journey
Into dry places called heartache and loneliness.

Forgiveness is the antidote to the bitter pill
It will heal you but you must let go of the past
Let God flush out those bad attitudes that clog your heart
His love will cleanse your soul of all of the trash.

Ask your Heavenly Father to send the living waters
Be quenched by His Spirit divine
Let His rivers renew your desert land
So the seeds of love can grow in time.

For love will heal the wounds of your bitter past
But you must be strong to not experience defeat
Let the rivers of joy flow from your heart
Because with God's love, life is...

Sweet.

"Then will I sprinkle clean water upon you, and ye shall be clean: from all your filthiness, and from all your idols, will I cleanse you. A new heart also will I give you, and a new spirit will I put within you: and I will take away the stony heart out of your flesh, and I will give you an heart of flesh."

Ezekiel 36:25-26

Amazing Grace

"When thou passest through the waters, I will be with thee; and through the rivers, they shall not overflow thee: when thou walkest through the fire, thou shalt not be burned; neither shall the flame kindle upon thee."
Isaiah 43:2

One day I had the honor of meeting a man who had fought in the Vietnam War. He told the story about a time when he was only 21 years old and in the fight of his life. He also talked about the bitterness that was harboring in his heart even though the war had long been over. The bitterness ate away at his heart because he had lost a leg during his service. It was a painful reminder of the tragedy that he and many others had experienced. For years he would replay the images of war over and over in his head. The mental anguish took its toil leaving him with so many unanswered questions. The war and its ill effects tormented his mind, body and soul for decades. He did not know if he could ever come to grips with the pain that it had caused.

Then one day he found what was missing from his life all those years. He realized that he was missing God's amazing grace and love. God's love came to him in the form of his son, Jesus Christ. Once he accepted Jesus as his personal Saviour, he found relief in the mist of the mental and physical storms. He was able to replace bitterness with forgiveness. He was able to come to terms with the war. The spiritual and mental battles only began once he had returned home from Vietnam. But through God's amazing grace and love, he was able to be victorious against the demons of depression and hurt. He is now armed with the Holy Word of God. Through his faith and trust in the Lord, he knows that his tormented soul will now rest in peace.

Are you living in a daily battle with the same demons of war that followed our brave soldiers home? If so, you must equip yourself with the Holy Word of God. He will be your shield and your help in times of trouble. He will heal your broken heart and mend your broken spirit. Let God cleanse your heart, renew your mind, and release you from the past. Read your bible today and pray for the strength to overcome. You are more than a conqueror through Christ Jesus whose loves you.

"Yea, though I walk through the valley of the shadow of death, I will fear no evil: for thou art with me: thy rod and thy staff they comfort me."
Psalm 23:1-4

Lost and Found

Lost...
In the jungle of turmoil and destruction
Lost in the thick marsh and overgrown wilderness
The battle fought in Vietnam was so long ago
But in my mind still lies the bitterness.

Lost in a world of screaming agony and pain
Lost of limbs, lost of blood, lost of precious lives
Shell-shocked by watching death walk over the land
Killing all people unmercifully as he sailed by.

Rewinding the scenes and running them through my head
I pray for relief but I am overcome with resentment
My heart is so full of hatred and despair
It must be purged so I can experience forgiveness.

So Lord, gather me now from this retched place
Cleanse me with the living waters of love forevermore
Renew my heart, my mind, and make me whole again
Release me from this terrible prison of war.

As I enter into your divine presence
Forgive me for the pain that I caused over there
For I was fighting for my beloved country...
My country, which I hold so dear.

But the price for the battle was too great
It has robbed me of so many years
It cost all of us love ones who died for glory
And left us trapped with memories of tears.

Lord, as I bow down to you wounded and heavy
Once again I put my life into your hands
As I did when I was amongst the killing fields
But this time help me to be born again.

My belief in you Lord grows stronger daily
I give to you the burdens that had me bound
Thank you for your love and for teaching me to forgive
I was lost but now Lord, I am...

Found.

Bondage in Sin

John 8:12

12When Jesus spoke again to the people, he said, "I am the light of the world. Whoever follows me will never walk in darkness, but will have the light of life.

Quality Control

I may not have control over my circumstances
For circumstances are as they are
Having already happened, I cannot change a thing
They are now beyond my control.

I may not be able to control my situations
Once they decide to take off
But I can control whether I allow myself to participate
Or whether I decided to just stay in the fog.

I may not have control over my children
After they reach a certain stage
But one thing that is for certain
They will be my children no matter what age.

I may not have control over my life
I am miserable because I will not change
I just keep doing the same old things
And I have only myself to blame.

I may not have control of the outcome
Once the outcome reveals itself
But before I reach that mark in my life
I better take a good look at myself.

I may not have control over many things
But I can control the quality of my soul
By confessing my sins and releasing the past
I must let Jesus take control.

"He that hath no rule over his own spirit is like a city that is broken
down, and without walls."
Proverb 25:28

A Spiritual Cleansing

Confession is good for the soul they say
It can relieve you from the anxiety
of being someone that you are not
You pretend that everything is fine
You play on other people's feelings
and yes, you even tell a lie or two
just to keep the facade going.
But inside you know that you are on fire
and it is getting hot in there
As the temperature rises with the truth
Like the sun rising on a cloudless day
across the desert sands
You sweat, you become profusely wet
Because you do not know when
your bubble is going to burst
But you got it under control
Or do you?

As the lies and the drugs become mountains
As the drinking and deceit become valleys
How high will you get?
How low will you go?
Will it take death to come knocking at your door?
What will it take for you to just say "No"?
Or will you be like many others who thought
This will not happen to me...
I can handle it...
What do they know...
It was only one drink, one hit,
that added up to more lies...
Will you make your mother cry?
Will her broken heart pay the cost in despair
Long after you have died?
But deep down under all the trash
Deep in your heart God's word was stashed

And when you had no where else to go
You remember that confession is good for the soul
And now that the weight has been lifted
give back what you have been given
Love, respect, trust, and hope
Never take for granted what God has given you
For as a vapor that vanishes quickly
so too will your life
And the Love that He has put in it
Is the greatest gift you will ever have
Be true to yourself and to God
And never be what others think you should be
God will direct your path
But it is up to you as to what road you will travel
Choose wisely.
Turn From Thy Ways

Past mistakes haunt you
As a parent you want the best for your child
But all they see as those mistakes repeat
Is how to just get by.

Bad habits slowly drain you
Sapping every chance to move ahead
They cause chaos and strain, confusion and pain
You should quit, but the habits continue instead.
Wandering eyes only find trouble
A lying tongue only bring hurt
A stony heart only reaps destruction
Instead of feeling better, you only feel worse.

Down the path that leads to sorrow
You still continue to stroll right along
Even though God tries to give you direction
You continue onward but He wants you to turn.

If you turn, He will remove from your shoulders
The chains that have you bound
Remove the things that you have been taught wrong
Remove the curses that have been handed down.

If you turn, He will break that cycle of shame
If you turn, He will break that cycle of pain
If you turn, He will break that cycle of pride
Turn to God and they will no longer remain.

Turn right now from thy wicked ways
Remove any iniquities that are holding you back
Be diligent in the task
To cleanse your temple at last
Speak to those hurts, those mistakes
Speak to those habits you must break
To make a change all it takes is a little faith
It is never too late to choose God's path.

"If my people, who are called by my name, will humble themselves
and pray and seek my face and turn from their wicked ways, then
will I hear from heaven ànd will forgive their sin and will heal their
land."
2 Chronicles 7:14

"Trust in the Lord with all of your heart, and lean not on your own
understanding; In all your ways acknowledge Him, and He shall
direct your paths."
Proverbs 3:5-6

The Answer Is Not In A Bottle

Why do you let the devil
Steal your joy from within
He tricks you all the time
In thinking the bottle is your friend.
That demon is taking your soul,
Your mind, your very being
You will let him take what is precious,
Your life...if you do not start seeing...

That the answers to your problems
Are not in a bottle or a glass
Seek the answers from the Lord
He is the only thing that lasts.

Alcohol will surely destroy you
It saps the very essences of your life
And the only things it leaves you with
Are pain, misery, and strife.
Your answer lies with Jesus
Give him your burdens and your cares
Believe that He will see you through this
It is your burdens He will bear.

For the word of God is powerful
It is sharper than any sword
It will cut the shame right out of you
Let your spirit be filled with His Word.
The Lord will never forsake you
He will meet your every need
According to His riches and glory
If you only start to believe.

That the answer is not in a bottle
Please let that demon move on
Put the Lord in your life now
He will carry you through the storms.

So when you are weak and lonely
Seek the Lord's strength to erase the pain
He will help you overcome your addiction
The answer: His love conquers everything.

"For the word of God is quick, and powerful, and sharper than any two-edged sword, piercing even to the dividing asunder of soul and spirit, and of the joints and marrow, and is a discerner of the thoughts and intents of the heart."
Hebrew 4:12

Just A Thief

Stick em' up! Oh, don't look now
Stick your hands high in the air
I am going to rob you of your time
This is a stick up but do not despair.

My name is not Johnny
Nor Billy, or Bob
It is Procrastination to you my dear
And stealing time is my job
So you really do not have nothing to fear.
I just came to rob you of your finances
Rob you of your health and peace of mind
I will steal opportunities and successes
I will steal your joy and rob you blind.

Nothing to fear you say? That is right!
Convincing you to wait will be so easy
All I have to say is a few little words
You will see that waiting is really very pleasing.

You can do it later!
Someone else will do it for you!
You work so much better under pressure!
So, what is the rush?
Why sweat the small stuff?
You will have more time to do it later!
In the meantime I am blocking your blessings
In the meantime I am stealing your peace
In the meantime you are getting overwhelmed
Don't you think it's about time you arrest this thief.

Lock Procrastination up
Throw away the key, in the dungeon he must go
Put the handcuffs on the one that is sneaking around
Who comes to steal, kill, and destroy.

Delays, debt, and denial are hazardous to your health
Get organized. Make some changes in your life
If you truly want success and happiness
Then you have to change to remove all the strife
But how? you may ask
Habits are hard to break and I have been this way all my life!
Are only excuses that will hold you back
You must give your problems to Jesus Christ.

You must pray to the Lord who can help you
Make God your first priority and then you will see
That His Word will give you the wisdom to recognize
That Procrastination is just a thief.

"I am the door: by me if any man enter in, he shall be saved, and
shall go in and out, and find pasture. The thief cometh not, but for to
steal, and to kill, and to destroy: I am come that they might have life,
and that they might have it more abundantly."
John 10:10-11

The Lost Generation

They shall be lovers of themselves
They shall be lovers of the world
They shall be disobedient to their parents
They shall be disobedient to God.

They shall lust after material things
They shall be full of envy and strife
They shall have no respect for authority
They shall have no respect for life.

They shall take all that they can take
And never give back anything
Never to work; never to grow; never to change
They expect to be given everything.

This is the generation that shall be saved
When Jesus gave us our mandate
Which is to seek and to save that which is lost
So that they will not pay the ultimate cost
For all of the love this world tries to take.

Therefore, search the kingdom for the lost
Search diligently; it is your assignment today
Knock on every door
Search high and search low
Give someone salvation
before it is too late.

"For the Son of man is come to seek and to save that which was lost."
Luke 19:10

Depression

Micah 7:7-8

[7] But as for me, I watch in hope for the LORD,
I wait for God my Savior;
my God will hear me.
[8] Do not gloat over me, my enemy!
Though I have fallen, I will rise.
Though I sit in darkness,
the LORD will be my light.

Comfort Me

As I lift my eyes up to the sky
I behold such a wondrous sight
Of beautiful clouds and a rainbow
Arching over a flock of geese in flight.

How high the mountains stretch upward
How vast the pastures roll
How bright the sunlight that pours down upon me
How magnificent God's creation unfolds.

When I think of all the goodness
When I think of all the joy
When I think of all the battles won
I thank God for saving my soul.

For I know He has shown favor to me
When I was sick and all alone
I know He placed his arms around me
When I was weak and feeling scorned.

I know that He has comfort me
When death knocked at my door
I know that He has sustained me
When I knew I could not make it anymore.

God created the tiny sparrows
And all other creatures, great and small
But when He created man and his woman
He showed us He loved us most of all.

By having His only son, Jesus
Die on the cross at Calvary
To pay for our sins and rise again
I knew in his heart He had a place for me.

So as I lift my eyes up to the sky
It is heaven that I am looking for
Until time is no more, my Lord will comfort me
To God be the glory
now and forevermore.

"Thou, even thou, art LORD alone; thou hast made heaven, the
heaven of heavens, with all their host, the earth, and all things that
are therein, the seas, and all that is therein, and thou preservest them
all; and the host of heaven worshippeth thee."
Nehemiah 9:6

Call To Duty For the Most High

Your mind is a battlefield
And the devil knows it
He lies in the trenches
Waiting to attack you
If your troops are not ready
Which are your thoughts
If your platoon is not equipped
Which is your body
If your commander is not ready
Which is your spirit
Then get ready for the fight of your life
Because the enemy is always seeking
That place of weakness that lies in your mind
He is looking to devour you
And he knows just where to start
He uses your past to weaken you
He uses family and friends to cut you down
He will use anything that will take your energy
He will use everything to take your focus from God
Therefore, you must put on your armour
You must be prepared
To do battle for the Lord; you must be aware
You must be strong to protect your heart
In order to dodge the devil's fiery darts
You must instill God's Word deep within you
You must be ready to be call to spiritual duty
In order to stand against the devil's plan of attack
Put on truth and righteousness for protection
Grab your bible, the Word, which is your sword
Draw into your soul the peace of God
Protect your mind with the helmet of salvation
And be filled with the Holy Spirit to survive
Guard yourself with love; always have your shield of faith
Be diligent to stand on God's promises which is your firm foundation
Keep your thoughts on the Word; pray without ceasing

Keep your eyes on God; it is his face you are seeking
No matter the pain or the price or the warfare in your life
Know that nothing is impossible for God
You will be the victor and the devil will be defeated
He will lick his wounds and go away for a season
He will lie in the trenches until another opportunity presents itself
For he wants to consume you
Fear not; be strong, for with God nothing can go wrong
Be always prepared and always pray to start your day
So that in every battle you are victorious
You are called to duty for the Most High
And you will never fight alone.

"Wherefore take unto you the whole armour of God, that ye may be able to withstand in the evil day, and having done all, to stand."
Ephesians 6:13

Valley Of Praise

I climbed up the mountain
To get to the other side
But all the effort I did by myself
Brought tears to my eyes
I need a healing for this body
That is full of sickness and pain
Seeing my tears the Lord said, "Follow me"
To a place where love reigns.
I descended to the place of victory
The valley of blessings, the valley of praise
The valley of rest and prosperity
The valley of healing
Where love showed the way
To the truth that points to salvation
Answered prayers, and mercy abound
The place where my heart is cherished
The place where Jesus is found.
I have come to rest from my labor
To be in the presence of the God I adore
I have descended into a holy place
To bring my petitions before my Lord
I am in need of a miracle healing
I am both physically and spiritually weak
But before I ask for a blessing
I must reverence the Lord that I seek.
I will glorify my Lord, I honor him
I bask in his Holy divine presence
For He is my Rock and my Strong tower
He is my Deliverer, He is my Defense
He is my Waymaker, He is my Provider
He is my hope, he is my peace
He is Lord of Lords, King of Kings
He is Jesus Christ, my mercy seat.
As I look to heaven from the valley
I see the glorious light of God's love

Shining down upon my broken body
Healing my spirit man with rain from above
Feeling rejuvenated and renewed
I praised God for all that He had done
You may have to climb a mountain
To get to the other side
But it's down in the valley where the victory is won.

"On the fourth day they assembled in the Valley of Beracah, where they praised the LORD. This is why it is called the Valley of Beracah(praise) to this day. Then, led by Jehoshaphat, all the men of Judah and Jerusalem returned joyfully to Jerusalem, for the LORD had given them cause to rejoice over their enemies."
2 Chronicles 20:26-27

Who Will You Serve?

My God is greater
than any problems I may have
He is greater
than all of my mistakes
My God is greater
than all of my sorrows
He is greater
than any trial that takes place
Failures may come
Tribulation will flow
Take it from me
for I surely know
That no matter the situation
No matter the pain
Where heartache reins
My God is greater.

He will never leave me nor forsake me
He will always show up right on time
He brings peace that
surpasses all understanding
I thank the Lord
that He's a friend of mine.
Did your god create the heavens?
Did your god split the seas?
Did your god die for your sins
on a rugged cross at Calvary?
Is your god there when you need him?
Can your god love you
unconditionally?

If "No" is your final answer
Do you have the faith to believe?
My God is greater
than any other god

My God is greater
than any problem left unresolved
He is greater than
any sickness or disease
Find out for yourself
or just take it from me
When all else fails
And there is no where else to turn
Have faith and believe
My God is greater.

"Declare his glory among the nations, his marvelous deeds among all peoples. For great is the LORD and most worthy of praise; He is to be feared above all gods. For all the gods of the nations are idols, but the LORD made the heavens."
1 Chronicles 16:24-26

Forsaken

Have you ever been hurt by someone
Who you thought you could depend on?
Have you ever been abandoned when times were rough?
Did your friends just run away when things got tough?
Have you ever been left all alone
When everything in your life seems to go wrong?
Have you ever been so filled with pain?
That your heart is broken from all the strain?
As you travel down the road of strife
Do you see support on your left and right?
If you cannot pray because you are ill
Do you have a friend who will?

Jesus knows about the pain you have
When friends forsake you when things go bad
For when He was ready to die upon the cross
He was forsaken just for saving the lost
The disciples were asleep during his time of need
One disciple denied his existence not one time but three
And one disciple betrayed Jesus for a bag of money
And the multitude said "Release Barabus", now isn't that funny
Jesus was forsaken emotionally by people who were his friends
He was forsaken spiritually even until the end
He was forsaken physically when the disciples fled
He was even forsaken verbally; "I do not know him" Peter said.

During great trial it is hard to imagine being left alone
During great trial it is hard to be forsaken when things go wrong
Even today in our daily walk we forsaken Jesus, our friend
By being ashamed to say we know him and never acknowledging
him
We forsake Jesus still despite the suffering He endured upon the
cross

We forsake Jesus even though for our sins He paid the ultimate cost
We may be going through trials and tribulations all by ourselves
But we are never truly forsaken; Jesus loved us like no one else.

"The LORD himself goes before you and will be with you; he will
never leave you nor forsake you. Do not be afraid; do not be
discouraged."
Deuteronomy 31:8

Disappointment

Job 33:27-29

[27]He looketh upon men, and if any say, I have sinned, and perverted that which was right, and it profited me not; [28]He will deliver his soul from going into the pit, and his life shall see the light. [29]Lo, all these things worketh God oftentimes with man...

Created In His Image

Reflections of long days
and fretful nights stare back at me
As I look into the mirror of my heart
I see loneliness, disappointments, and pain
I see fear lurking in my every thought.

A prisoner of my own self-image
A prisoner of unrealized dreams
A prisoner of expectations and worldly perceptions
The fear of rejection keeps me bound in chains.

"I am not good enough"
"No one loves me"
"I am not pretty enough"
"No one cares"
"I am not smart or courageous or strong enough"
"I am not important"
Why should God answer my prayers?

Then a friend one day said something
That would break this cycle of self doubt
She said "You are a child of the Most High
God loves you for who you are therefore do not pout!"

You must defeat the devil
when he enters into your mind
Because all he brings is negative things
You have to start to believe
that you were made in the image of God
Be blessed by God's love and the joy that it brings.

You are your own worst enemy
When you allow the devil to enter your thoughts
Because he will only plant seeds of destruction
It will destroy your self esteem
It will destroy your heart.

Remember what the Bible tell us
that in God's image we were wonderfully made
He will dwell with us for a lifetime
Never leaving us nor lead us astray.

In His image we are a royal priesthood
In His image we are God's heirs
In His image we are blessed beyond measure
Do not be deceived, God will answer your prayers.

Therefore, release yourself from your prison
Use God's Word to restore your heart and mind
So that you can see that you are a beautiful creation
Not from the world's image but in the wonderful image of God.

"So God created man in his own image, in the image of God he
created him; male and female he created them."
Genesis 1:27

One Sunday Morning

One Sunday morning as the sun begin to shine
And the dew gently rested on the meadow
A young woman decided that it was time
that she got her life together.

Her mind and body showed the signs
Of a life that was filled with sin
She was an alcoholic, she did many drugs
She sold her soul for love to strange men.

This particular morning brought her little peace
For death stared back at her in the mirror
She knew that this fight had to cease
If she was going to get any better.

But sin had a hold of her
It did not want to let go
She knew it was taking its toll
But her will to change was gone.

She prayed that God would show her favor
If she would repent her wicked ways
And she made a promise to get dress and go
To church on that very day.

As she entered into the doors
There were whispers and many stared
For no one could believed that this woman
Would show her face in there.

Instead of embracing her and welcoming her in
They immediately started to say
How can this woman who is so full of sin
Turn from her wicked ways?

Instead of feeling discouraged
The young woman had a promise to keep
Which give her the strength to be encouraged
To go to the altar and fall on her knees.

She asked the Lord to renew her spirit
To transform her mind, body, and soul
She asked the Lord to remove from her
The sins that had her in bondage for too long.

She said, "Lord, I give my life to you
Despite what others say
I know you have a plan for me
Please work a miracle today.

I know there will be struggles
And I know there will be trials
But having you as my Lord and Savior
Will make it all worth while.

I came to you wounded and afflicted
You received me when no one else would
I have been redeemed by your saving grace
You saved my life when no one else could".

Salvation delivered her from darkness
So with boldness she made this plea
She told the congregation to never forget
God still works miracles for those who believe.

"Create in me a clean heart, O God: and renew a right spirit within me. Cast me not away from thy presence; and take not thy holy spirit from me. Restore unto me the joy of thy salvation; and uphold me with thy free spirit. Then will I teach transgressors thy ways; and sinners shall be converted unto thee."

Psalms 51:10-13

"For you created my inmost being; you knit me together in my mother's womb. I praise you because I am fearfully and wonderfully made; your works are wonderful, I know that full well."

Psalms 139:13-14

Resting Place

One precious seed falls softly to the ground
It finds a place to lay and takes root
In time it springs forth and become
one of God's creations, the dandelion.

As the dandelion floats from one field to the next
So does the lost who do not have Christ in their life
For without Him they may travel endlessly
And like the dandelion, they may travel alone.

On this particular day, the breeze is gentle
the dandelion calmly comes to rest on a blade a grass
It is a peaceful place, tranquil and quiet
green meadows and golden rays of sunshine.

It reminds us of the place God has in our hearts
One of safe haven and a place of refuge
A resting place full of hope and love
A place to lay when our journey comes to an end.

As time moves on, the winds change to a turbulent pace
Tossing the dandelion to and fro,
blowing it into frightening, scary territory
It lays open to the elements which causes pain and harm.

Our lives travel the same hard and winding road
At times the trials seem to come all at once
But with God's grace and love we can survive
Just like the dandelion, we travel by faith...we must go on.

Battered and bruised, the dandelion once again
is swept into the air refresh and renewed
But this time the sun shines on a brand new day
It rejoices and dances with morning's sweet dew.

So shall we praise the Lord when He bless us
with another opportunity to see the new morn
So shall we thank the Lord
when He gives us His undying love
Just like the dandelion onward we must go
So keep pressing through the storms of life
For we are all God's creations, great and small
He has a resting place for us all
Heaven is its name.

"Sing, O heavens; and be joyful, O earth; and break forth into
singing, O mountains: for the LORD hath comforted his people, and
will have mercy upon his afflicted."
Isaiah 49:13

Seasons Come, Seasons Go

The seasons change before our eyes
Hues of yellows, browns, and reds
blanket the autumn sky
As God paints such a beautiful canvas
Need we ask why
Because this earth is God's creation
Seasons come and go as time passes by.

For nothing will last forever
Eventually everything must die
The trees, the flowers, each blade of grass
must follow each season that God provides
And as for us whom God love the most
Because of Calvary we do not have to ask why
So make each and every moment count
before time passes you by.

Spring blends into summer
Summer rolls into fall
Fall gives way to winter
Winter is the coldest of all.
The seasons pass before our eyes
But we still live our lives the same
We do not grow in our spiritual walk
We do not make a change.

We live as though tomorrow is guaranteed
Need we ask ourselves why
Because we have taken this life for granted
But just like the leaves, we eventually die.
Therefore, make that life changing decision
Just do it now. Do not ask why
Give it all to Jesus, your Lord and Savior
before He comes back and passes you by.

"To every thing there is a season, and a time to every purpose under the heaven:"
Ecclesiastes 3:1

Tender Moments Like These

I looked up into the balcony
And there you were
Dressed to the nines
Looking so proud and happy
As I crossed the stage
To receive my diploma.
At that very moment
I knew that I would not have
Made it this far
If it had not been for your love.

When I had my daughter
And then my son
You were right there cheering me on
Even though my life was little chaotic
You did not give up on me.
Instead, you told me to press
Because life will give you trials
It will test your faith.
At that moment
I prayed that I would have
The inner strength
That God had blessed you with.

Even when you lost your husband
Your only love, my father
You reminded me that life is what you make
That even when sorrows come
You must keep your eyes to God
And everything else
Will take care of itself.
Right then, at that very moment
I prayed that my faith
Would be made stronger
And over the years, it has.

Dear Mother,
You have always been the inspiration
That I needed to keep my boat in the water
To keep my sail up
And to keep moving in God's direction
Despite the storms that may rage in my life.
I want to thank you for that.
But most all, I want to thank you
For your love and support
That filled my life
With tender moments like these.

"Thy father and thy mother shall be glad, and she that bare thee shall rejoice."
Proverbs 23:25

Discouraged

Job 30:25-27
[25] Have I not wept for those in trouble?
Has not my soul grieved for the poor?
[26] Yet when I hoped for good, evil came;
when I looked for light, then came darkness.
[27] The churning inside me never stops;
days of suffering confront me

Saved By His Grace

I had a long talk with my Lord one night
Drowning in my sorrows, doubt and shame purged my light
My heart was so heavy, my soul was in pain
Crying out in the dark
So unbearable was the strain.

Shaking, shivering in anguish
I laid down my every burden
As I poured out my soul
wails of hurt overflowed each realm.

Oh Lord, I cried, please rescue me
for I am broken beyond repair
Please rekindled the flame of my eternal light
Then the voice of the Lord answered my prayer.

"My dear child, you are more precious to me
then all the riches on earth
You are so important to me
for I have known you before your birth.

I am thy God Almighty
There is nothing I cannot do
I am thy Lord Omnipotent
Nothing is more stronger than my love for you.

Alone, you poured out your tears to me
So I will remove your misery and pain
But you must give your life to me
And ask for peace in my Holy name".

The hold of my struggles loosen its grip
For in the eternal darkness, I saw a great light
Bowing down to His Holiness with tears in my eyes
I gave the Lord my all, I gave Him my life.

As I relinquished my spiritual being
I saw my burdens lifted up and carried away
what a sweet relief that engulfed me
As the dark of night gave way to day.

Salvation had visited me that very night
Love rekindled the flame that once ceased
Joy has replaced my sorrow
No worries for tomorrow
For in God, I have found perfect peace.

"For by grace are ye saved through faith; and that not of yourselves:
it is the gift of God:"
Ephesians 2:8

Unanswered Prayers

You prayed and you pray again
But there is no relief in sight
You lift your hands up to thank the Lord
You say a prayer each and every night
You read God's Word
You go to church
You try your best to live a Christian's life
But your prayers keep going unanswered
Even though you have prayed
with all of your might.

You wonder what are you doing wrong
You wonder why you are not getting blessed
You begin to notice that everyone else
Is making it through their test
You wonder why you are having so much pain
After all, you try to do what the Bible said
You wonder if your prayers are in vain
Did God not listen to what you said?

Maybe you are being disobedient
In the areas you want to be blessed
Maybe you are asking the Lord to do something
That you are not ready to do just yet
Maybe you are not waiting patiently
To see if God will answer your plea
Maybe He is trying to work things out
Orchestrating your blessings behind the scenes.

Sometimes God will respond
With an answer that we do not want to hear
Sometimes God will respond
But we miss out because of our fears
Sometimes God will respond
But our faith has gone astray

God will respond because He wants to bless you
As long as you try to do things God's way.

Therefore, reevaluate how you pray to Him
Give God your all, your soul, and your mind
Then just have faith, believe, just wait and see
God will answer all your prayers
Right on time.

"If my people, who are called by my name, will humble themselves
and pray and seek my face and turn from their wicked ways, then
will I hear from heaven and will forgive their sins and will heal their
land."
2 Chronicles 7:14

Hide and Seek

Hide...

The Holy Word of God deep within your heart
And lean not unto your own understanding
For the instructions that the Bible impart
Will protect and guide you when life is demanding.

Search for the truth; rightly divide the Word
Apply it to your life and put it into action
Let your deeds and your works speak loud and clear
May the examination of your life give a positive reaction.

Find the time to pray to your Heavenly Father
Make time to kneel before His glorious throne
Bring to Him your burdens; leave them on the altar
Repent your sins to Him; confess all of your wrongs.

Explore the Word to see what the Lord has done
For you will find you can do all things through Him
Look for gems of wisdom that will strengthen you
Within each verse it proves that Jesus is your friend.

Conceal in your heart all the promises of God Almighty
Read the Bible and apply each verse every day of the week
To grow in grace and in the full knowledge of Christ Jesus
It is the face of our Lord and Saviour that you must diligently

Seek.

"Then shall ye call upon me, and ye shall go and pray unto me, and I
will hearken unto you. And ye shall seek me, and find me, when ye
shall search for me with all your heart."
Jeremiah 29:12-13

"When thou saidst, Seek ye my face; my heart said unto thee, Thy face, LORD, will I seek. Hide not thy face far from me; put not thy servant away in anger: thou hast been my help; leave me not, neither forsake me, O God of my salvation."
Psalm 27:8-9

Wait On The Lord

Wait on the Lord for his guidance
He will never forsake you nor lead you astray
When you need a helping hand
You can depend on Him always.

Wait on the Lord for He will listen
Knock on His door, then ask, and you shall receive
When you need someone to talk to
Just pray to the Lord while on bended knees.

Wait on the Lord for His perfect strength
His power will help you endure what life can bring
When you are feeling timid and very weak
With him you will sail on eagle's wings.

Wait on the Lord for everlasting peace
For His peace surpasses all understanding
When you are dealing with tribulation
His peace will be with you when life is demanding.

Wait on the Lord for compassion
For He is with you, He is closer than a brother
When you are lonely and friends forsake you
In God, you will find no other.

Wait on the Lord for patience
He will help you but you must wait
When you are upset and full of turmoil
He will answer your prayers but you must have faith.

Wait on the Lord for abundant joy
It will shelter you from the misery and pain
When you are full of deep sorrow
With the morning light a new day you will gain.

Wait on the Lord for healing
For with Jesus stripes and your faith to believe
When you are dealing with sickness and hurt
It is miracle healing that you will receive.

Wait on the Lord for deliverance
He will deliver you from every situation
When you cry out to ask his forgiveness
Praise the Lord! Give thanks for his every action.

Wait on the Lord for the things that you seek
Do not rush through for it is you that He adores
Wait on the Lord for his love is everlasting
Wait, I say, wait on the Lord.

"I wait for the LORD, my soul doth wait, and in his word do I hope."
Psalm 130:5

Witness

To be a faithful witness
A chosen people, holy and dear
You must clothe yourself accordingly
With loving care and the right gear.

You must put on your full armor
To prepare for the warfare of sin
You must start with the word of God
And let it strengthen you from within.

Cover yourself with kindness and compassion
Dress yourself with meekness and humility
Make sure you are gentle and honest
Then put on patience and then you will see...

That there is a daily battle
One that you can not win
You will experience pain and frustration
If you are not ready to fight against sin.

So put on the belt of truth
For all of the struggles you will meet
Put on the breastplate of righteousness
And the gospel of peace fitted on your feet.

Then carry the shield of faith
To protect you from hurt and harm
Then put on the helmet of salvation
Bring the sword of the Spirit under your arm.

The Lord has provided instructions
His Word will be your guide
But if you do not take time to study
You will surely begin to back slide...

Into foolish talk, pride, and envy
Slide into anger, unhappiness, and pain
You must prepare to do battle daily
Or you will live your life in vain.

So do clothe yourself accordingly
By praying always and living the Word
For you are His chosen people
Be a witness for the Lord.

"We pray this in order that you may live a life worthy of the Lord
and may please him in every way: bearing fruit in every good work,
growing in the knowledge of God."
Colossians 1:10

Fear

Psalm 27:1-2
[1]The LORD is my light and my salvation; whom shall I fear? the LORD is the strength of my life; of whom shall I be afraid? [2]When the wicked, even mine enemies and my foes, came upon me to eat up my flesh, they stumbled and fell.

Safe In His Arms

I feel your loving arms around me
I feel your hands catch me when I fall
I know that you are with me always
Your presence surrounds me from dusk to dawn.

You are Almighty, you are Glorious
You are Wonderful, You are God
You are so powerful and so faithful
I know I am safe within your arms.

You are worthy of all of my praise
I bow down on my knees in reverence to you
I close my eyes just to listen to your tender voice
Oh Lord, I want to hear from you.

I can rest assure that you will lead me
I can rest assure that you will guide my path
I can rest assure in the promises of eternal life
I believe in my heart that your love will last.

When I am feeling down, you lift me up
When I am weary you send peace to me
When I am feeling weak and so alone
Your arms give me strength to have faith and believe.

You are my strong tower
My refuge to protect me from harm
You are my Rock that no weapon can form against
No matter where life takes me, I am safe in your arms.

"I will heal my people and will let them enjoy abundant peace and
security."
Jeremiah 33:6

"Praise the Lord, O my soul, and forget not all his benefit — who forgives all your sins and heals all your diseases."
Psalm 103:2-3

Traveling Mercy

It is common practice for people to ask the Lord for traveling mercy. Depending on things like the mode of transportation, whether it is a holiday, vacation, or just driving to and from work, many people pray for safe travels. But when they travel on the highway called life, many do not seek the Lord's protection along the way. The world is full of avenues where you can encounter many obstacles that will cause major detours. Sometimes these detours can draw your life into unfamiliar territory that can cause great pain and anxiety. But the Lord will provide the guidance that one needs to get back on the right path. His mercy and grace endures forever. It is God's compassionate love that saves us from destruction. You may not know what lies ahead but God already knows what is in store. He will never lead you astray. All you need to do is listen to the Lord and do his perfect will. Open your heart and your mind to God. Take time to pray for traveling mercy before you start a new day. By allowing God to direct your path, his love will protect you from danger seen and unseen. Thank you Lord for traveling mercy.

"If I take the wings of the morning, and dwell in the uttermost parts
of the sea;
Even there shall thy hand lead me, and thy right hand shall hold
me."
Psalm 139:9-10

As I travel on this highway called life
I ask that you watch over me dear Lord
For I know the roads are treacherous
And full of unexpected detours.

I ask for your divine mercy
As I travel along each path
Send your angels to camp around me
For your protection I know will last.

A fork in the road, a few side streets
Unfamiliar territory, I am lost and confused
Hear my cries oh Lord, guide me I pray
Help me back to the place of refuge.

Lord, grab me when I go astray
From the narrow path of righteousness
Hold me tight when danger comes into view
Safe and secure, I know I am blessed.

As I travel on this highway called life
Over mountains high and valleys low
Thank you Lord for traveling mercy
And for your love that saved my soul.

"Not by works of righteousness which we have done, but according
to his mercy he saved us, by the washing of regeneration, and
renewing of the Holy Ghost; Which he shed on us abundantly
through Jesus Christ our Saviour;"
Titus 3:5-6

Peace Be Still

When the storms of life are raging and my ship is battered, beaten and torn, I find myself in a desperate search for peace. Life can bring so much chaos and turbulence that many find it hard to bear. If you could escape from it all, which route would you take? Some find solace in prayer, where others revert to smoking, drinking, bingeing on food, or doing drugs. The latter can cause heartache, anger, and pain, which only add to their daily, never ending frustration. It is time to choose the route that will lead you to every peaceful solution for every turbulent situation. It is time to choose the path that leads to God.

To have peace in your life, you must have the Lord in your life. Begin today by spending a few minutes in prayer and meditation with the Lord. You will find a refuge of tranquility with the Lord. He will provide the inner peace that your spirit needs. If you believe in your heart and confess with your mouth that Jesus is Lord, you will find peace that will transcend all understanding. Invest your time in Him today and peace will be your reward.

"And the peace of God, which passeth all understanding, shall keep
your hearts and minds through Christ Jesus."
Philippians 4:7

When the storms of life are raging
Say, "Peace be still".
When the winds of adversity are blowing
Say, "Peace be still".
When the waves of tribulation try to overtake you
When the downpour of problems floods your soul
Know that Jesus is your anchor
Say, 'Peace be still".

"And he arose, and rebuked the wind, and said unto the sea, Peace, be still. And the wind ceased, and there was a great calm. And he said unto them, Why are ye so fearful? how is it that ye have no faith?"
Mark 4:39-40

As For Me And My House

As for me and my house
We shall faithfully serve the Lord
With a loving, grateful heart
As a family in one accord.

As for me and my house
We shall praise His holy name
We shall study His holy Word
For it is salvation that we shall claim.

As for me and my house
We shall diligently pray
Giving thanks before our God
This will be our custom every day.

As for me and my house
We shall count it joy when trials come
For thy Spirit is within these walls
And our home is build by His love.

As for me and my house
We shall faithfully serve the Lord
For without Thee we are nothing
His peace is with us forevermore.

"Choose for yourselves this day whom you will serve…but as for me
and my house, we will serve the LORD."
Joshua 24:15

Thought of the Day

Sitting,
pondering what life would be like
if I did not know
God.
It is a depressing
almost suffocating feeling
of despair that takes over
the moment
I surrendered to that thought.

I would be tossed
like a lost ship on a
stormy sea
rain beating my brow
whipping my outer shell
into ciaos bruised inside
damaged beyond repair.

If God
was not in my life
that means the enemy
feeling elated
was once again ruler
over my life
ruler over my thoughts,
my words, my deeds, my actions
allowing him to reek havoc
on myself and on
all those around me
allowing sickness, worry,
heartache and pain
Oh my...
Frightened by the very thought
of not having salvation
of not being free in the Holy Spirit

But being held captive
by the enemy that drains
all the joy, all the love, all the peace
from my spiritual being
I bind that thought in the name of
Jesus Christ
my Saviour and my Redeemer
never to wonder
for I am saved from sin
never to ponder
that thought ever again.

"Casting down imaginations, and every high thing, that exalteth
itself against the knowledge of God, and bringing into captivity
every thought to the obedience of Christ."
II Corinthians 10:5

Evening Prayer

O, merciful God, whose name is above all names
My Lord, my Saviour, my Redeemer, my friend
I give you all the honor, the glory, and the praise
As this long, eventful day draws to an end.

I thank you for my health and for my family
I thank you for the peace that you bring
You helped me through each stressful hour
I give you praise for everything.

As the moon glides into the dark sky
As the stars begin to shine so deep
Forgive me, Lord, for all my shortcomings
Tears of repentance fall down my cheeks.

I magnify you Lord, oh how I love Thee
Because of your unfailing grace I can rest easy
Renew my spirit; restore my soul tonight
And if tomorrow does not shine its morning light
I am truly blessed indeed.

"I will both lay me down in peace, and sleep: for thou, LORD, only
makest me dwell in safety."
Psalm 4:8

Treasure Beyond Measure

As dark days fell upon my brow
Clouds of fear, anxiety, and pain thus form
It is difficult to fathom why this is happening to me
My strength dims beyond measure
I am so weak and worn.

Within the darkness lies so much pain and suffering
Within the darkness so much heartache and strife
Within the darkness so much loneliness and despair
Lord, I need a breakthrough to heal my life.

"What you feel are treasures of darkness
Do not let it distract you from what is in store
For riches reside in the most secret of places
Have faith and I will take you there"
Thus saith the Lord.

"I will take you to a place of comfort
A places filled with tranquility and love
A place where only your heart can lead you to
A place where light shines with hope from above".

You will never experience the faithfulness of God
If you have not gone through some suffering and pain
He will deliver you from your bondage
Through God's grace and mercy
He summons you by name.

"When I call you, seek my face and you will find the riches
That will make you whole once more
For I will never give you more than you can bear
Be healed for I am God"
Thus saith the Lord.

"And I will give thee the treasures of darkness, and hidden riches of secret places, that thou mayest know that I, the LORD, which call thee by thy name, am the God of Israel."
Isaiah 45:3

Guilt

Job 11:13-18

[13] "Yet if you devote your heart to him
and stretch out your hands to him,
[14] if you put away the sin that is in your hand
and allow no evil to dwell in your tent,
[15] then you will lift up your face without shame;
you will stand firm and without fear.
[16] You will surely forget your trouble,
recalling it only as waters gone by.
[17] Life will be brighter than noonday,
and darkness will become like morning.
[18] You will be secure, because there is hope;
you will look about you and take your rest in safety.

Detoxify My Soul

Fast to remove all the impurities
Of this world's toxic activities
Remove the guilt from your life
Remove the criticism, remove the strife
Purge from the wasteland all the trash
Remove the grudges of the past
Remove the blame for things gone wrong
Remove unforgiveness; you must be strong
For the cleansing process is a painful one
It will hurt to change but you have begun
By identifying these areas that hold you back
Know that the Bible provides your plan of attack
So ask the Lord to give you a clean heart
Ask for a clean slate, ask for a new start
Instill into your heart love and peace
Instill in your mind to pray without cease
Instill into your being compassion and hope
Let God's Word and his love purge your soul
Plant within yourself his righteousness
Reap in mercy so you can be blessed
Seek the Lord for the ultimate fast
Because only what is done for God will last
Detox your soul today.

"Create in me a pure heart, O God, and renew a steadfast spirit
within me. Do not cast me from your presence or take your Holy
Spirit from me. Restore to me the joy of your salvation and grant me
a willing spirit, to sustain me."

Psalm 51:10-12

Cup of Life

As frustration pours into my cup
It begins to overflow from the constant rain
Splashing out as it hits
The stress, the disappointments, and woe
It brings turmoil; it brings pain
Over whelmed by the sheer weight
It reaches its breaking point
My cup slowly begins to leak
Here and there
It begins to crack under pressure
But I will not let it go
Instead of pouring out this burden into God's hand
I hold on to it with fear and with pride
Hold on to the pain, the suffering
For I did not want anyone to know I was weak inside
My cup becomes heavier
My hand becomes weak
It beckons to the Lord's plea
"Give me your burden, pour your cup out to me"
Then my cup tips over and slips out of my hand
It shatters as it hits the ground
The fragments of its life
Scattering around, spiraling down
But they are caught by the hands of God
As He separated each fragment
From the hurt and the pain
He handles each gently
Then like a potter with his clay
He begins to mend my broken pieces
Putting them back together again
With his love and his grace
He strengthens my cup with his tender mercies
As the new dawn takes over the place
He washes my cup whiter than snow
With his blood He removes my sins

With his power he restores my soul
With his love he made me whole
Then He begins to pour in his peace
That surpasses all understanding
He poured in his hope
He poured in his grace
He poured in faith
But when He poured in his Holy Spirit
My cup was transformed
Then he took my cup and placed it in his right hand
Holding it so gently, delicately, with love
With his right hand he protects
My cup from the elements
From the wind and from the rain
From the pain and the suffering
Daily He allows me to take my cup back
And once again frustration flows in
But this time my cup is a little stronger to with stand
The pressures that life has to give
Because when I pray all those burdens just fade away
And once again my cup is renewed
I can never repay the debt Jesus paid for me
Way back, long ago at Calvary
No matter how many dents, bumps, or scratches there may be
Thank you Lord for my cup of life.

"I love the LORD, because he hath heard my voice and my
supplications.
Because he hath inclined his ear unto me, therefore will I call upon
him as long as I live.
The sorrows of death compassed me, and the pains of hell gat hold
upon me: I found trouble and sorrow. Then called I upon the name
of the LORD; O LORD, I beseech thee, deliver my soul. Gracious is
the LORD, and righteous; yea, our God is merciful.
The LORD preserveth the simple: I was brought low, and he helped
me.

Return unto thy rest, O my soul; for the LORD hath dealt bountifully with thee.
For thou hast delivered my soul from death, mine eyes from tears, and my feet from falling. I will walk before the LORD in the land of the living.
I believed, therefore have I spoken: I was greatly afflicted:
I said in my haste, All men are liars. What shall I render unto the LORD for all his benefits toward me? I will take the cup of salvation, and call upon the name of the LORD.
I will pay my vows unto the LORD now in the presence of all his people."
Psalms 116:1-14

Medication for the Soul

Humor me, please tickle me
Make me laugh today
Because laughter is the best medicine
To chase the blue away.

Calm your fears and renew your faith
Be happy you are alive today
Take plenty of time to share a smile
Take time to laugh and play.

On this day make plans to be happy
For tomorrow may never come
Ask the Lord to give you a joyful heart
Before this day is done.

Think on things that will bring you peace
Do not worry: do not fret
Let go of the problems and give them to God
Then you will find the road to happiness.

Laughter is the best medicine
To soothe your heart and soul
It takes your mind off of the pain
It replaces sunshine for the rain
Enjoy each moment before it is gone.

"Blessed are ye that hunger now; for ye shall be filled. Blessed are ye
that weep now; for ye shall laugh."
Luke 6:21

"For his anger endureth but a moment; in his favour is life: weeping
may endure for a night, but joy cometh in the morning."
Psalm 30:5

Before The Well Runs Dry

Emptiness casts a shadow
Upon my beaten brow
My body shows signs of the battle
Of long, hard days gone by.

Loneliness fills my empty heart
I feel the hush of the cold air
Shivering I cannot feel the warmth
That use to be there.

I can only see the water before me
I can hear its crashing waves
I am drowning in self-pity
As sorrow's tide begins to rise.

I look up to see a wondrous light
I stretch my hands out to Thee
I call upon his name for help
Lord Jesus, my Saviour, my King.

He calmed the storm; He calmed the sea
He rescued me from the rain
Then He filled my heart with his love
I was made whole once again.

He saw within me a drop of faith
As those long, hard days went by
Sometimes it takes a tear or two
Sometimes you have to cry
Sometimes you will reach the breaking point
Sometimes you will wonder why
Just make sure you always call on God
Before the well runs dry.

"Counsel in the heart of man is like deep water; but a man of understanding will draw it out."
Proverbs 20:5

Call On Jesus

Dear Lord,
As I enter your gates with thanksgiving
As I enter your court with praise
I am bringing to you my petition
To help me escape from darkness today.

Yesterday, I was thrown in the dungeon
Because I was found guilty of sin
I fell so hard that when I looked up
It was the deepest hole that I ever fell in.

I can see there is a flicker of light
Shining right above my head
But I allowed negative thoughts to hinder me
Instead of reaching up, I looked down instead.

The shame, the guilt, the anguished
Was a great weight that had me bound
I knew that I had totally messed up
Because my life was now turned upside down.

Can I not make it back to you dear Lord?
Can you forgive me Oh Lord I pray?
Can you see in my heart that I repent dear Lord?
Can you bring me back to you this very day?

Prayer is the key to break the shackles
Faith is the key to release your pain
Put pride aside and love yourself enough
To call on Jesus glorious name.

Call on Jesus when you are feeling low
Call on Jesus when life takes its toil
Call on the glorious name of Jesus Christ
Whether it's noontime or in the darkest of night

Never think you have fallen so far away
That Jesus cannot rescue you today
You are redeemed from your bondage of pain
Just look up and call on
The matchless name
Jesus.

"Hear me when I call, O God of my righteousness: thou hast enlarged me when I was in distress; have mercy upon me, and hear my prayer. O ye sons of men, how long will ye turn my glory into shame? how long will ye love vanity, and seek after leasing? Selah. But know that the LORD hath set apart him that is godly for himself: the LORD will hear when I call unto him. Stand in awe, and sin not: commune with your own heart upon your bed, and be still."
Psalm 4:1-4

Gift of Love

Do you have a dad that knows the Lord
And can see the power of His might?

Do you have a mom that seeks His face
Does she live by faith and not by sight?

Do you have a brother who reads the Word
And lives by its caring ways?

Do you have a sister who loves the Lord
And prays to Him everyday?

Do you have an aunt who cares for you
And keeps the Lord first in her life?

Do you have an uncle who teaches you
Using the Lord's instructions
To show you what's right?

Do you have grandparents who go to church
To praise His glorious name?

Do you have a cousin who sings of His grace
And treats everybody the same?

Do you have a husband who is the head
But let the Lord guide him on the right path?

Do you have a wife who is precious and kind;
Is her life an example that one should have?

Can you then look at yourself and know that you
Have been given a gift from above?

For if you have family like this in your life
Then God has blessed you with the greatest gift
Love.

"For God so loved the world, that he gave his only begotten Son, that whosoever believeth in him should not perish, but have everlasting life."
John 3:16

Hatred

Matthew 6:22-24

[22]The light of the body is the eye: if therefore thine eye be single, thy whole body shall be full of light.

[23]But if thine eye be evil, thy whole body shall be full of darkness. If therefore the light that is in thee be darkness, how great is that darkness!

[24]No man can serve two masters: for either he will hate the one, and love the other; or else he will hold to the one, and despise the other. Ye cannot serve God and mammon.

Let Us Love One Another

When I think about all of the violence that transpires in this world of ours, it is amazing that our Lord is such an awesome and forgiving God. When we remain divided by race, creed, religion, and color, we loss favor with our Heavenly Father. Nothing is gained because this division breeds hatred, malice, and strife. It keeps us from growing together in God's love. We must put away our old selves and love one another with the same conviction that God loves us. Then maybe this world will become a better place for all people for generations to come. But until we look beyond the differences that we can see and start searching for the beauty that is within, we will always have racial and social problems to contend with. We are all children of God. Nowhere in the Bible does it mention that one race or color is more important to Him than another. We all were created equal in the eyes of the Lord.

The tragic events that took place on September 11, 2001 will forever be part of our legacy. Hatred and envy transformed the destructive forces that devastated our lives that day. Life is like a vapor that can vanish before our eyes. Which is way we must hold life dear and treasure every moment that we have. For the evils of this world have come to kill, steal, and destroy. But we must not let our hearts be trouble for the day of the Lord is nigh. The battle against these terrifying forces belongs to the Lord and we must trust him to do his will.

Therefore, it is time we love our brothers and sisters no matter what their backgrounds may be. For when we stand before God, we are all the same. The color of our skin will not matter. How much money we made will not matter. Our background and status, our name or religion, will not matter on judgment day. The only thing that will matter is that you loved your neighbor as yourself and that you lived your life fully for the Lord. How does your chapter in the Book of Life read? Do you love your fellow man? Do you love the Lord with all of your heart? Remove the shackles that tear us apart

and tell someone you love him or her today. The love of God will
bond us together. Let nothing separate you from God's love.

This story is dedicated to those who morn the lost of love ones on
September 11, 2001.

"These things I spoken unto you, that in me ye might have peace. In
the world ye shall have tribulation: but be of good cheer; I have
overcome the world."
John 16:33

"For I am persuaded, that neither death, nor life, nor angels, nor
principalities, nor powers, nor things present, nor things to come,
Nor height, nor depth, nor any other creature, shall be able to
separate us from the love of God, which is in Christ Jesus our Lord."
Romans 8:38-39

Songs of Freedom, Carry Me Home

Expressions of deliverance
Spirituals of hope and faith
Melodies coming down from heaven
Songs of a love so great.
Steal away into the night
My faith looks up to Thee
To keep me safe from hurt and harm
As I begin this long, hard journey.

A journey to freedom, to the Promised Land
Over Jordan is where my heart will be
Searching, longing, for His grace and mercy
My Lord watches over me.
The spirituals were messages of hope
The spirituals spoke of death and of life
The spirituals sent a message of victory
The spirituals helped us to overcome strife.

If you listen very closely you can hear the angels sing
"Wade in the water, wade in the water children,
Wade in the water, God's gonna trouble the waters".

If you listen very closely you can hear them warn
"Hush, hush, somebody callin' my name
Hush, hush somebody callin' my name
Oh my Lord, oh my Lord, what shall I do".

If you listen very closely you can hear them sing
"Swing low, sweet chariot, coming for to carry me home
Swing low, sweet chariot, coming for to carry me home".

Traveling over mountains high and through valleys low
Via the Underground Railroad we did not stray
Traveling to freedom with a song in our heart
With God guiding us every step of the way.

When we finally cross over Jordan to the Promise Land
And see our Lord and Saviour face to face
Overcoming social injustice, pain, and suffering along the way
We know we have come this far by faith.

After we have overcome, after we have won this race
Rejoicing in victory, you will hear us sing:
"My eyes have seen the glory of the coming of the Lord
His truth is marching on".

Glory Hallelujah to our Lord and Saviour
Glory Hallelujah for the spirituals, for the songs
Glory Hallelujah for our freedom, our life
Our Lord is coming back to carry us home.

A Time To Heal

From the fiery pit to a place of refuge
Thy Lord will protect thee forever more
Thy hand will lift thee up from this world of iniquity
His grasp is firm, He will never let go.

As grief and sorrow burns deep within
The scars of life's battles now must heal
Though pain and affliction brings weeping once again
Time moves on even when it seems to stand still.

Thy eyes hold sorrow in its stare
Thy heart is broken beyond repair
Thy memories are filled with tears to share
Oh Lord, shelter thee with Thy love and care.

Thus the pictures of smiles and joy delight
Reflections when life was so grand
Wiped out by one tragic moment in time
Lord, remove such hatred from the hearts of man.

From the beginning our Lord gave us a choice
To live our lives with compassion and love
Praise God who gives grace unto the humble
As you mourn pray for those who persecute us.

For time will tell the story of strength
It will show that perseverance is God's will
Be patient and know this battle is not yours
Thy Lord will be victorious, America
Take time to heal.

"Be ye also patient: stablish your hearts: for the coming of the Lord
draweth nigh"
James 5:8

"Because of his strength will I wait upon thee: for God is my defence"
Psalms 58:9

Mission of A Lifetime

Years have passed
        since you last seen my physical man
And yet, you still believe
        in the mission God placed upon my heart
That mission has always been a simple one
        But it was held hostage by hatred from the start.

It was intended to ignite the flame of love
        that will glow throughout all generations
But due to the coldness of one's heart
        and the hatred of one's soul,
It was almost extinguished by my assassination.

But with the grace of God and His protective angels
        Our Lord did not let the waters of hate overflow our land
He was with us as we flowed through the rivers of adversity
        He had carried us when we could no longer stand.

I tell you now be not afraid
        for I have seen the Promised Land
And even though I said I may not make it there with you
        I know that God has prepared a place
And He has you included in His marvelous plan.

So let my life continue to be a reminder
        That no matter the situation, no matter the pain
No matter the trials and tribulations that may come your way
        With God by your side, you can conquer anything.

Set your mind on things that are not of this world
        Believe in your hopes and in your dreams
But above all, let peace and love prevail
        So that my life and the live of others will not be lost in vain.

Mine eyes have seen the glory,
         your eyes will see it too
But first you must love one another
         And let God's love bind those that may hate you.

Years have passed since you last seen my physical man
         To my family and friends, stand firm and be strong
Dr. Martin Luther King, Jr. is my name
         God will remove the hatred and the pain
            Have faith and know that our victory is won .

"Now our Lord Jesus Christ himself, and God, even our Father, which hath loved us, and hath given us everlasting consolation and good hope through grace, Comfort your hearts, and stablish you in every good word and work."
2 Thessalonians 2:16-17

Defining Moment

For every circumstance, for every season
That draws us closer to our Lord and Saviour
There may be pain, there may be sorrow
But with God's omnipotence there is hope for tomorrow.

One tragic moment in time defined our stance
It defined our faith to stand on God's promises
We must believe that He will bring us through
Lord, we know we must put our trust in You.

For every mountain that may stand in our way
For every turbulent sea with it's crashing waves
God's love for you will not be shaken nor fail
He will protect you, He will keep you safe and well.

One moment in time defined our strength
To withstand devastation and unhappiness
It defined our ability to carry on despite the fears
It defined our perseverance despite all of the tears.

It defined our lives which now has changed forever
One moment of destruction showed us what really matters
We must love one another and let all hatred cease
Lord, we pray the next moment
Will bring us Your love and peace.

One moment to live, one moment to die
One moment that will forever bring tears to our eyes
May His love sustain you in your time of sorrow
Because with God there is always hope for tomorrow.

"Though the mountains be shaken and the hills be removed, yet my
unfailing love for you will not be shaken nor my covenant of peace
be removed," says the Lord, who has compassion on you."
Isaiah 54:10

Peace in the Midst of War

Why must there be death and destruction?
War raised its ugly hand
So that the mighty will rule the weak, he replied
And let terror consume the land.

Why must the innocent be slain for progress?
War answered with all of its fear
So that hearts can be violently broken
And oppression can consume the tears.

Why must our soldiers die, why must our mothers cry?
Why must our freedom be buried with our sons and daughters?
So that the cause is worth the sacrifice, War said
And so that boundaries will be apart much farther.

Why must we forget what devastation bring?
Why do we not learn from past mistakes and cease?
War replied, because your eyes are on this world's rewards
And not on God who will bring you peace.

"Depart from evil and do good; seek peace, and pursue it."
Psalm 34:14

Insecurity

Psalm 43:2-5
2 You are God my stronghold.
Why have you rejected me?
Why must I go about mourning,
oppressed by the enemy?
3 Send forth your light and your truth,
let them guide me;
let them bring me to your holy mountain,
to the place where you dwell.
4 Then will I go to the altar of God,
to God, my joy and my delight.
I will praise you with the harp,
O God, my God.
5 Why are you downcast, O my soul?
Why so disturbed within me?
Put your hope in God,
for I will yet praise him,
my Savior and my God.

Woman of God

She is more precious than rubies, more finer than pearls
She spends her entire life studying God's Holy Word
She gains strength from the Lord to fight the sins of this world
She is an instrument of God: She is a prayer warrior.

She is a righteous woman
A daughter of the Most High
A woman of God
That's she.

She seeks the Lord in prayer with great spiritual passion
She is fully committed to God's plan for salvation
She is willing to sacrifice all of her worldly possessions
She beams a heavenly light in her style and her expressions.

She is a majestic woman
A daughter of the Most High
A woman of God
That's she.

She always seeks a quiet place to show God reverence
She longs to enter into His holy presence
She faithfully serves the Lord and stands by His promises.
She loves the Lord with her heart and through Him, she's victorious.

She is a spiritual woman
A daughter of the Most High
A woman of God
That's she.

She presses towards the mark for the edification of Christ
She is devoted to teach the gospel for the rest of her life
She brings forth joy and thanksgiving that is well-pleasing in God's
sight
She is ordained by the Holy Spirit to preach His word day and night.

She is a virtuous woman
A daughter of the Most High
A woman of God
That's she.

"Let your light so shine before men, that they may see your good
works, and glorify your Father which is in heaven."
Matthew 5:16

Legacy of Love

Dearest Mother,
Do you know how much you mean to me?
Do you know how much I care?
Have I told you lately how much I love you?
Have I told you that you are in my prayers?

Your legacy of love was placed on a foundation
Built by God's love, mercy, and grace
You always knew how to make our home stable
You knew with God's help, we would win this race.

You taught us to always keep our heads held high
You reminded us that we were heirs to the throne
Even when times were hard and we were poor
You told us to keep the faith when things went wrong.

You showed us that sometimes the storms would rage
And that there will be sorrow to make us cry
Which is why you taught us to live our lives fully
And to not let God's blessings pass us by.

Dearest Mother,
In the darkest of night you prayed for us
And by day you tenderly shaped our very being
Our lives would have turned out so differently
If you did not believed in us to succeed.

You chastised us to remind us to be a Christian example
You scolded us in order to learn right from wrong
You wanted God's love to shine brightly within us
For we are God's children, we are heirs to His throne.

Dearest Lord,
Thank you for letting me be my mother's child
Thank you Lord for all the sacrifices she has made

Thank you for sustaining her through all her sufferings
Thank you for bringing her happiness to replace the pain.

Dearest Lord,
You always remind us that tomorrow may not come
For there are mothers who already sang their farewell song
There have been opportunities to say I LOVE YOU
That were regretfully missed and now those moments are gone.

Which is why I want to tell you, dear Mother
My love for you grows stronger each blessed day
Tears of joy flow as I give honor to our Lord for you
I love you, Mom, now and for always.

Daughter of the Most High

Daughter, you are the precious jewel of my being
When I look at you I see myself
Young, venerable, and inexperienced
And yet, I know that with God's help
My prayers for a better life for you
Will be answered in time.

You struggle with the changes of growing up
With adulthood, you have blossomed
Into a majestic rose of Sharon
Your beauty is one to behold
And yet, you do not see your blessings
Because you are blind.

Not blind in the physical sense
But blind to what God has for your destiny
You do not live your life fully for the Lord
You have instead chose to take the hardest path
You became a single mother at such a young age
To raise a child alone, it will take a strong mind.

The anxieties, the anguish, the frustrations
Leaves you hanging your head low
The burden of all the new responsibilities
Leaves you struggling to make it alone
But you are not alone in this world
For you have a friend who is loving and kind.

That friend is named Jesus
Go to Him when you need refuge from the storm
Call on Him when you need a helping hand
Study and live by His Word when raising your child
You are a daughter of the Most High
And I thank God that you are a daughter of mine.

"I have no greater joy than to hear that my children are walking in
the truth."
3 John 1:4

The Beauty In Me

Why can I not see the beauty in me?
    Is it low self esteem or insecurities?

When I look in the mirror I feel somewhat deceived
    Because the beauty in mc is not what I see.

How can I mend my heart that has been
    So battered and bruised by the pain from within.

If I cannot love myself who can I love then,
    when I think I am not good enough for my family or friends?

I ask You dear Lord, how can I be strong,
    when my life is in shambles and everything is wrong?

Where do I go when all hope is gone?
    Why must I feel that I am so all alone?

God gave His answers to all of my insecurities
    He said I must love myself and have faith to believe,

That He has blessed me with life more abundantly,
    And through His love I can see the beauty in me.

"Whose adorning let it not be that outward adorning of plaiting the hair, and of wearing of gold, or of putting on of apparel; But let it be the hidden man of the heart, in that which is not corruptible, even the ornament of a meek and quiet spirit, which is in the sight of God of great price."
1 Peter 3:3-4

Love Me For Me

When you look at my big thighs, my large breasts,
My round after my momma's derriere
See beyond my physical being
And start looking at the beautiful spirit within me.

When you hear me talk about my day, about my stress,
And about the plans that I made
See beyond the words that you hear
And just listen to how I feel.

When you see my curly hair, my big brown eyes,
My not a size 6 body size
See beyond my voluptuous stature
And just support me no matter.

When you touch my mind, my loving heart,
With words that only tear me apart
See beyond your judgmental ways
And know the damage you bring is not ok.

So when you tell me you care about my health,
About my self, and my happiness
See beyond what you think are my faults
Open your eyes and please examine your heart
Know that I'm a beautiful woman of God that you see

Accept who I am
Love me for me.

"For with what judgment ye judge, ye shall be judged: and with
what measure ye mete, it shall be measured to you again."
Matthew 7:2

A Mother's Heart

Like sheer crystal glass, my heart is fragile
Shattered, broken, would my heart be
My love for my children runs so deep within
To endure such loss; O Lord, please spare me.

My children are the love of my life
They bring joy and hope for tomorrow
They are my ultimate blessings from God
To lose them would bring such sorrow.
In the Lord's hand, He holds their future
And in His arms, He keeps them safe
He is their provider and Maker
He gave them to me to nurture with grace.

I know that someday they will depart
Unto life's highway of bumps and curves
But I know that the Lord will guide them with
Directions to fly on the wings of His Word.

My children are my heart's desire
To think of them just brings me to tears
O Lord, you are an awesome God
To have blessed me with children so dear.

"Her children arise up, and call her blessed: her husband also, and he
praiseth her."
Proverbs 31:28

Loneliness

John 12:45-47
[45]When he looks at me, he sees the one who sent me.
[46]I have come into the world as a light, so that no one who believes in me should stay in darkness.
[47]As for the person who hears my words but does not keep them, I do not judge him. For I did not come to judge the world, but to save it.

Missing You

I miss your touch, your sweet caress
I miss your smile and your tenderness
I miss the way you stroke my hair
I miss your loving care.

When I look into the sky I see your face
When I feel the sun I feel your warm embrace
When I close my eyes it is you that I see
Oh how I wish you were here with me.

My heart just aches for you my dear
I miss you so much it brings me to tears
Until time can erase the miles between us
May God bless you always,
I miss you my love.

"I opened to my beloved; but my beloved had withdrawn himself, and was gone: my soul failed when he spake: I sought him, but I could not find him; I called him, but he gave me no answer. The watchmen that went about the city found me, they smote me, they wounded me; the keepers of the walls took away my veil from me. I charge you, O daughters of Jerusalem, if ye find my beloved, that ye tell him, that I am sick of love."
Solomon's Song of Songs 5:6-8

A Father to the Fatherless

As a single mother the task of raising my children
Is one of hard work and stress every day
For it requires a great deal of strength
To make sure they are cared for always.

I worry about them not having their father
Because he has decided to move on again
The unhappiness I see in their eyes
Makes me wish I had done better for them.

Then one day I met a dear friend
Who knew someone who would supply all of our needs
She said he was very kind and gentle
But I must give my heart to him willingly.

She said he would be a loving father
She said he would never leave us at all
She said he had an only begotten son
Who died and rose again a short time ago.

As I listen to her describe this person
The more I heard, the more in love I became
I got so excited about actually meeting him
I had to ask her for his first name.

She smiled and said His name is Jehovah
He is the lover of your soul
He is the ultimate provider and comforter
And you can call him Lord.

He will be the role model that your children need
And He will bless you beyond measure
He will be your friend in times of trouble
He will love you now and forever.

So be patient and wait on the Lord
He will send you a good man someday
But as for your children, worry not
He is the Father to the fatherless for always.

"And will be a Father unto you, and ye shall be my sons and
daughters, saith the Lord Almighty."
2 Corinthians 6:18

God Intended for Us To Meet

God has a way of letting us know that He is there for us

Sometimes you can hear Him in your heart if you listen

Sometimes He can use other people to come into your life

I believe that it was meant for us to meet

It is no accident that I am in your life nor you are in mine

God intended for us to meet.

I just want you to know that you have a friend in me

I understand what you are experiencing in trying to reach your goals

I will support you every step of the way

I speak of God always because He had brought us through tough times

He has blessed you and I with happy times.

It is because of Him that we are alive today

I am truly glad I had this opportunity to know you

You will always be in my prayers and my thoughts

The minutes spent with you are precious and few

But the minutes spent with God is time well spent

He loves us both unconditionally

There's no greater love than He

And I love you my friend dearly as you have loved me

God intended for us to meet

To seek His goodness and mercy no matter

Because if neither one of us did not have God in our life

We probably would not have been together
God intended for us to meet.

"Beloved, let us love one another: for love is of God; and every one
that loveth is born of God, and knoweth God. He that loveth not
knoweth not God; for God is love."
1 John 4:7-8

Most Precious

Your love and friendship means the world to me
More precious than silver or gold
You are a wonderful person whom I come to believe
That God sent you for me to know.

You are easy to talk to when I am feeling down
More precious than diamonds or pearls
You are strong when I am weak and bound
You help me survive in this crazy world.

You give of yourself with no strings attached
More precious than money or things
You are a beautiful creation of the Lord
Stay as you are; please do not change.

You are a friend during my time of need
More precious than riches or wealth
For these things cannot replace love you see
Or bring to my life any happiness.

You are sweet, loving, caring, and kind
More precious than status or fame
I am so glad you are a friend of mine
You stood by me through my joys and pain.

So I want to thank you for your love
More precious to me than you will know
You are truly a blessing from heaven above
To my best friend, I love you so.

"She is more precious than rubies: and all the things thou canst
desire are not to be compared unto her."
Proverbs 3:15

The Visit

As I look outside my window
anticipating for the time to come
Oh what joy is sent from heaven above
When my friend comes to the nursing home.

She brings songs of glad tidings
She brings stories of days gone by
She brings activities to keep us busy
She brings a smile that can light up a sky.

There have been many times I wondered
why she comes here every week
After all, I am not her relative
but she is a dear friend to the meek.

What happiness she showers upon us
What love she brings to brighten our day
The Lord has truly blessed us
We thank God for her kindness in every way.

Although I am no longer able
to do all the things I once did back then
If there will be a bright spot in my life
It is when she comes to visit again.

"The hoary head is a crown of glory, if it be found in the way of
righteousness."
Proverbs 16:31

You Are My God

Sometimes when I am all alone
I go to my Father
I bow at his throne
Praying fervently, please hear my plea
Remove this pain Lord; please rescue me
I'll give you the glory
For your power will reign
I'll get down on my knees again and again.

You are the joy of my life
You are the reason I'm alive
You are my strength when I'm weak
You are the hope that resides in me.

You are my shelter in time of need
You are Holy; you are majesty
You are my peace; you are my love
You are my help
You are my God.

Sometimes when I'm on a raging sea
The wind, the driving rain overpowers me
I must have faith of a tiny seed
My God can move mountains
But I must trust and believe.

You are clothed in righteousness
You are the reason I withstand the test
You are the hope that resides in me
You are my shelter in time of need
You are Holy; you are majesty
You are my peace; you are love
You are glorious, You are divine

You are with me for all times
I am never alone
You are my God.

"The Lord reigneth, he is clothed with majesty; the Lord is clothed
with strength, wherewith he hath girded himself: the world also is
established, that it cannot be moved. Thy throne is established of
also; thou art from everlasting. The floods have lifted up, O Lord, the
floods have lifted up their voice; the floods lift up their waves. The
Lord on high is mightier than the noise of many waters, yea, than the
mighty waves of the sea. The testimonies are very sure; holiness
becometh thine house, O Lord, forever."
Psalm 93

The Meaning of Friendship

Friendship...
Unconditional love the transcends space and time
No barriers can hold back the feelings that two hearts share
No walls between you that can stop the flood of emotions
that will spill into each waking moment
For we are one; we think alike, we laugh, we cry,
We forgive and we are forgiven
For we overlook each other faults
and we see each other's needs
Caring about the spiritual well being
the physical condition, the mental state, the soul
We see each other for who we are
Beautiful, brilliant, resilient, and kind
Being there in silence and being there
in sorrow, wiping the tears away
giving a shoulder to lean on; holding on;
clinging for dear life in search of strength
To be carried through trouble waters
and to be lifted high above adversity
even when you are down
Giving encouragement go the next level
The ultimate cheerleader... "You can do it; have faith!!!"
Always there and there is no place else you rather be
But be with your friend, right there by their side
To dwell in your heart and mind for eternity
To never let the world come between you
For what you have is like a rare jewel
Precious and true
And together you can conquer the world
Together you will fly on the wings of love
for you are destined for a heavenly journey
with the only true friend that loves you both
Unconditionally
And his name is Jesus
Our holy example of pure love

Who gave his life for a friend so that each one would be saved
To give love and to have love
No strings attached
Friendship.

"A man who has friends must himself be friendly, But there is a friend who sticks closer than a brother."
Proverbs 18:24

To Love, Honor, and Cherish

On this day we made a vow to love one another
To honor and respect, to cherish each other from the start
We made a promise to be there through good times and bad times
Until our deaths only then we shall part.

We must now be strong against principalities
We must be diligent about our quest
To survive through all the dark days ahead
God will shine through the clouds; our marriage is truly blessed.

We must communicate to one another
We must be helpful in times of need
We must be honest about our shortcomings
We must accept each other's faults and believe...

That our love is stronger than temptation
That our love is stronger than strife
That our love will last through the generations
Because we have the Lord first in our life.

Before God and our family we promised
To love, honor, and cherish always
Until the last breathe has left our lips
This promise begins on our wedding day.

For every circumstance and for every season
We will work hard to make this be
The most happiest days of our life
It is God's plan for us to succeed.

We must be patient with one another
We must raise our children with a loving hand
We must be united in every situation
We must have trust as our new life begin.

We were two people who came together
To be one flesh in the sight of our Lord
therefore we will not let man separate us
For we are joined forevermore.

Through health and pain, joys and sorrows
He wants us to cherish every moment we know
We will honor one another for always
And with His love our marriage will grow.

"And they twain shall be one flesh: so then they are no more twain,
but one flesh. What therefore God hath joined together, let not man
put asunder.
Mark 10:8-9

The Birthday Prayer

The Lord looked down from heaven on the day of your birth
And realized that this day was yours to be introduced to Earth
He breathed his Holy Spirit into your being and thus your life began
You were wonderfully made and filled with his love right then.

But he knew you were entering a perilous world
A world full of danger; one with pain that can be so cruel
So to protect you, to watch over you, to keep you safe in his care
When you wake to see a new morning, start it by saying this prayer;

Lord, I thank you for another day to see your heavenly work
I give you the honor and glory for all my days here on Earth
I thank you for my parents and for my family
I thank you for all the blessings that you have bestowed upon me.

You have been a solid foundation when times have been so hard
You helped me through all my trials; because of you I've come this far
I thank you for your love and for the peace you bring to me
I thank you for this day for it is one I may not have seen.

I thank you for my birth and all the days I've enjoyed since then
I look forward to another year full of hope to grow within
I know I will not live forever but with you I know I can
Look forward to life eternal guided by your unchanging hand.

So Lord, I thank you with all my heart for my special day
As I continue on my journey forgive me if I should stray
I know I am your child and I thank you for my life
For today and every day is my birthday, thanks for making it so right.

So as I end this prayer of thanks I want to tell you now
That my life is stronger because I know that you are around
You have given to me a chance to see a brand new day
And I will always give you the honor, dear Lord, I pray.

So the best of everything to a very special person indeed
May the Lord bless you always with love more abundantly
May you see his beautiful glory and feel his peace in every way
My prayers are with you always
Happy, Happy Birthday!!!

"My son, forget not my law: but let thine heart keep my
commandments: For length of days,
and long life, and peace, shall they add to thee."
Proverbs 3:1-2

Rejection

Romans 8:34-35
[34]Who is he that condemns? Christ Jesus, who died — more than that, who was raised to life — is at the right hand of God and is also interceding for us. [35]Who shall separate us from the love of Christ? Shall trouble or hardship or persecution or famine or nakedness or danger or sword?

Separate But Blessed

A new year is upon us
A time for change
A time for dedication
A time for declaration
A time to take a stand
Upon the Word of God
And be separated from the world
Like Jesus.

I am different
Separate by the love of my Lord and Saviour
He already established my boundaries
In him, my limits were already set
To not go where man always go
But to go only where God wants me to go
I am separate; yet I am blessed.

I am appointed
By God's love and his mercy
To be determined to walk by faith
To be determined to live by grace
To be determined to shine in his glorious light
To be determined to be victorious to win this race
During which I will be persecuted; yet I am blessed.

I am ordained
Because God has made a way for my gifts
To be used to bring glory to his kingdom
I am a willing vessel; a living sacrifice
To seek and save that which is lost
For the ministry God has indwelled within me will shine
Therefore, whatever I do in word or deed
I do all in the name of Lord Jesus
I will have opposition; yet I am blessed.

I am changed

143

Because of God's Word
I will never be the same again
For I am now separated from this old world
A world that I ask
Where is the peace that surpasses all understanding?
When talk of war is all I hear and see
A world that I ask
Where is the joy, unspeakable joy?
When there is great sadness throughout humanity
A world that I ask
Where is the love; the undying, uncompromising love?
When hate is flowing so free.
This is a world that came gladly exclude me
I am excluded; yet I am blessed.
I am cleansed
For God's word has touched my heart
It has cleansed my thoughts
It has purified my soul
It has sheltered me from the storm
It has strengthen me to go on
It will remove from me any spiritual decay
It will separate me from all evil ways
I have been washed in the blood of Jesus
I am purged; yet I am blessed.

I am the sheep of God's pasture
What can separate me from his love?
Not perils, nor hardships, not heights, nor depth
Not angels, nor demons, not life nor death
According to the Word of God not one thing
Can separate me from Jesus, my Shepard, my King
For that I will have tribulation; yet I am blessed.

I am a servant
A faithful servant; resolved in doing God's will
When Jesus separates us upon his return
In his right hand is where I want to be
For I want to inherit the kingdom

That my heavenly Father has prepared for me
I will keep my eyes steadfast on Him
To remove any distractions that will take my mind off of Him
I may be estranged from family; I may even lose friends
Because I can no longer hang out in this world full of sin
I will even be chastised; yet I am blessed.

I am compelled
To tell somebody
About God's love and his Holy Spirit divine
In this New Year I will be diligent
To give God more of my time
I will separate myself as thus saith the Lord
And conform not to this world's plans
For no matter what the challenges are
On Christ the solid rock I will stand
With God's Word I am prepared for the test
With God's word I will persevere
In this I can surely rest
Apart from this world I can abide in Christ Jesus
I may be separate
I may be excluded
I may have trials
And even be persecuted
In spite of it all
Whether I walk or whether I fall
In God
I am truly blessed.

"Blessed is the man who perseveres under trial, because when he has stood the test, he will receive the crown of life that God has promised to those who love him?"
James 1:12

Identity Crisis

Jesus was despised and rejected
Unchanging, Jesus knew what He stood for
Uncompromising, Jesus knew in his heart who He was
Created in God's likeness and not the image of the world's.
So ask yourself the following questions
To see if you have compromised
If you find yourself answering yes
Then you may want to ask yourself why.

Do you have to talk a certain way
to be included with the crowd?
Do you have to dress a certain way
to be accepted at all?
Do you wear your hair in the latest styles
because that is what the celebrities do?
Do you have to be a certain weight
and give up certain foods?
Do you have to lie about who you are
or where you reside?
And while your heart is breaking
do you just smile when you need to cry?
Do you strive on people's expectations?
Do you seek the approval of man?
Do you live in fear and alienation?
Do you waver, bend, or
do you take a stand?
Do you think if you are not living like the Jones
that you are not worth nothing at all?
Do you buy material things you cannot afford
while robbing Mary, Peter, and Paul?
Do you have a life that is in turmoil
because of the status that you seek?
Do you have a life that is empty?
Do you have a life that just reeks?

If your answer is yes to most of these questions
An identity crisis is taking place
You are allowing the world to shape you
To mold you
Against the image that God has put in place
You are beautiful without the makeup
that hides the features God's blessed you with
You are handsome when you wear clothes
That are modest and that actually fit.
You are smarter when you live by God's Holy Word
than living by the latest slang
You are much brighter when you step out on faith
Rap may be cool but sing a song of praise.

You are victorious in every battle
whether it is financially, spiritually, or other wise
Do not worry about material things
Your needs will be met; God will supply.
Do not seek the adoration of man
For you will find disappointment waiting for you
Seek only the things of God
And He will surely bring a blessing to you.
Do not fear rejection from your peers
Believe what the Bible says who you are
You may even be despised and rejected like Jesus was
But never, ever forget
You are a child of God.

"So God created man in his own image, in the image of God created
he him; male and female created he them."
Genesis 1:27

_____

The Lost Generation

They shall be lovers of themselves
They shall be lovers of the world
They shall be disobedient to their parents
They shall be disobedient to God.

They shall lust after material things
They shall be full of envy and strife
They shall have no respect for authority
They shall have no respect for life.

They shall take all that they can take
And never give back anything
Never to work; never to grow; never to change
They expect to be given everything.

This is the generation that shall be saved
When Jesus gave us our mandate
Which is to seek and to save that which is lost
To gain back the hearts that Satan tries to take.

Therefore, search the kingdom for the lost
Search diligently; it is your assignment today
Knock on every door
Search high and search low
Give someone salvation
before it is too late.

"For the Son of man is come to seek and to save that which was lost."
Luke 19:10

The Forward Prayer

Lord, help me to go forward
To live up to what you expected
So that I can become a better person
Instead of someone left behind and rejected.

Lord, I want to go anywhere but backwards
I want to break this cycle of shame
I want to only live for your glory
To walk the right path in Jesus name.

Lord, when the devil show the old photos
of times of pain, doubt, and despair
Help me tell him the past does not matter
Because you always answered my prayers.

Lord, as I put the past behind me
I can see a brand new day
Full of life, love, and happiness
With my eyes on you each step of the way.

Lord, as I now go forward
I know I can win this race
For the prize of the high calling
Is what I strive towards before it is too late.

For time waits for no one
And tomorrow may never come
Which is why I must live my life fully
With the Lord first before it is done.

So Lord, thank you for your mercy
And for your patience in waiting to see
That I will live up to my full potential
So others can know my testimony.

Lord, I will go anywhere but backwards
Because of your love I already know where I have been
I look forward to all of your blessings
My destiny is your home called Heaven.

Lord, giving you honor, glory, and praise
For all that you have done
In Jesus name, I pray this forward prayer,
Amen. The victory is won!

"Brethren, I count not myself to have apprehended: but this one
thing I do, forgetting those things which are behind, and reaching
forth unto those things which are before, I press toward the mark for
the prize of the high calling of God in Christ Jesus."
Philippians 3: 13-14

A New Beginning

Lord, I come to you a broken spirit
Wounded by life's battle with sin
I must confess that my heart is aching
I must repent; I must be cleansed.

A new beginning, a fresh new start
A new commitment to press towards the mark
For I am a sinner saved by grace
I give you my life so I can win this race.

I give to you all of my storm clouds
I give to you my hurts and pains
I give to you all of my burdens, my trials
For your love will never change.

A new beginning, a fresh new start
A new commitment to press towards the mark
For I am loved beyond all measure
A love that out shines all earthly treasures.

I may be broken; I may be hurting
I may be wounded beyond repair
But I know that with each day you give me
You will not give me more than I can bear.

A new beginning, a fresh new start
A new commitment to press towards the mark
For by the stripes of Jesus Christ, I am healed
On Thy Word I will stand and will do Thy will.

A new beginning, a fresh new start
A new commitment to press towards the mark
For I am healed; Hallelujah, I am saved
To God be the glory, the honor, and the praise.
Amen.

"Heal me, O Lord, and I will be healed. Save me, O Lord, and I will be saved, For you are the one that I praise."
Jeremiah 14:17

At The Feet of Jesus

Come and worship at the feet of Jesus
Come and bring to him your burdens and cares
For Jesus is the healer and He want to make you whole
So bring him your broken spirit and leave it there.

Come and worship at the feet of Jesus
Come and listen diligently to his every Word
Do not let the cares of this world keep you too busy
Be like Mary and spend time with the Comforter.

Come and worship at the feet of Jesus
Bring to him your alabaster box full of your very best
Bring your finest ointments to honor him
Wash his feet with your tears; bring him nothing less.

Come and worship at the feet of Jesus
Touch the hem of his garment and see a miracle start
Get so close to him that your life will be changed forever
Bow down before him and He will give you a clean heart.

Come and worship at the feet of Jesus
Come right now; do not wait another day
Behold how He loves you so dearly
For all that He has done
To Jesus, give him the glory, the honor, and the praise.

"And she had a sister called Mary, which also sat at Jesus' feet, and heard his word. But Martha was cumbered about much serving, and came to him, and said, Lord, dost thou not care that my sister hath let me to serve alone? bid her therefore that she helps me. And Jesus answered and said unto her, Martha, Martha, thou art careful and troubled about many things: But one thing is needful: and Mary hath chosen that good part, which shall not be taken away from her."
St. Luke 10:39-42

"And behold, a woman in the city, which was a sinner, when she knew that Jesus sat at meat in the Pharisee's house, brought an alabaster box of ointment. And stood at his feet behind him weeping, and began to wash his feet with tears, and did wipe them with the hairs of her head, and kissed his feet, and anointed them with the ointment...And he said to the woman, Thy faith hath saved thee: go in peace."
St. Luke 7:37-38, 50

"And a certain woman, which had an issue of blood twelve years...When she had heard of Jesus, came in the press behind, and touched his garment. For she said, If I may touch but his clothes, I shall be whole."
St. Mark 5:25, 27-28

154

Wonderfully Made

You fashioned me in my mother's womb
With your glorious Spirit my tapestry was designed
You create a beautiful, one of a kind, embroidery
An original creation was what you had in mind.

All the days of my life were written in your heavenly book
Before time had a story to tell
My path was laid out like the patchwork of a loving quilt
Each block of fabric was carefully measured so well.

Woven together by the threads of your holy word
Knitted together by your peace and love
Every strand that was used to make me strong
Binds the material of hope from heaven above.

The talent you gave me was that of a tailor
One who sews and designs fashions for a living
But I see in it your wonderful handiwork
For this talent is also a ministry of giving.

As I look at my own unique designs
Each one tailored only for that person's size
I see that you did the same for each one of us
When you created our hearts and our lives.

I toil over each aspect of the garment at hand
Like you did when you made me that day
You knew exactly how the outcome would be
So I pray that my work reflect you always.

For I sew with love and joyous abandonment
Since I want each piece to fit just right
Like when you created us as our own unique tapestry
To be true and holy in your precious sight.

But as time tells our life story
There are days when our threads are so frail
That is when you renew our jagged edges
When you answered each one of our prayers.

So Lord, continue to use me as you see fit
For I am here to humbly serve you today
I thank you for creating me in my mother's womb
Because of your love, I am wonderfully made.

"For thou hast possessed my reins: thou hast covered me in my
mother's womb. I will praise thee: for I am fearfully and
wonderfully made: marvelous are thy works: and that my soul
knoweth right well."
Psalm 139:14-15

Sickness

Isaiah 58:8-9

8 Then your light will break forth like the dawn,
and your healing will quickly appear;
then your righteousness will go before you,
and the glory of the LORD will be your rear guard.
9 Then you will call, and the LORD will answer;
you will cry for help, and he will say: Here am I.

More Than A Conqueror

Over whelmed by the constant fear
That this disease will consume my life
I cannot even bring myself to call its name
For like a bird flying free anxiety will take flight.

I cannot speak about the loneliness
Or that my body is racked with pain
I cannot speak about this feeling of worthlessness
For I know I will be healed in Jesus name.

But the devil continues to bring the thoughts
That I shall soon see my life come to an end
For he is trying to convince me that I have lost
The battle against cancer, a battle I cannot win.

Tears run freely into heartache's stream
Which begins to overflow making my body shiver
Why, oh why dear Lord did this have to happen?
How can I fight what seems to be a losing battle?

He reminded me that I have a God who is faithful
Who has supplied my needs and answered my prayers
He will sustain me even through this difficult time
My faith cannot falter for I know that He cares.

My faith will not falter because His Word is true
All I have to do is believe it and He will release
His almighty healing power to strengthen me
All I have to do is speak of His peace.

So instead of asking why, I asked to survive this test
I asked that God's healing power descend upon me
I asked that His saving grace make me whole again
And I told the devil that he could not have me.

Through my faith that was as small as a mustard seed
I prayed into existence my healing through His Word
And even if I do not see tomorrow
Today in Christ Jesus, I am more than a conqueror.

"Nay, in all these things we more than conquerors through him who
loved us."
Romans 8:37

His Holy Presence

Before you make your request be made known
Enter into the holy presence of the Lord
Exalt His glorious name on high
For He is worthy to be praised and adored.

Show reverence; fall down upon your face
Be still and listen diligently for His word
Clear your mind, your heart, and your soul for blessing
Be humble when you are in the presence of the Lord.

When you pray to the Master bow down and know
That your request will be heard for sure
You must have faith to leave your every burden
Faith is the key that opens prayer's door.

Thy Lord is with you through the end of time
He will sustain you when you are weak and frail
He will comfort you in times of trouble
He will heal the sick; He will answer your prayer.

He is a loving and merciful God
Who loves his children more than we will ever know
We must make time to pray to our heavenly Father
We must take time to read His Word.

We must ask for forgiveness for our shortcomings
We must be thankful for every need that is met
Pray that the Lord will give us strength to survive
Honor Him with thanksgiving for promises kept.

Magnify the Lord for His name is above all names
Sing hallelujah for He is the Omnipotent One
Pray to the Father, the Son, and to the Holy Ghost
In heaven and here on earth, Thy will be done.

"But thou, when thou prayest, enter into thy closet, and when thou hast shut thy door, pray to thy Father which is in secret: and thy Father which seeth in secret shall reward thee openly."
Matthew 6:6

Someone is Praying for You

The Lord knows your every pain
There is none He cannot heal
He knows your deepest sorrows
There is none He cannot feel
Be not afraid to ask Him
for He already knows your every request
Enter into your prayer closet and join Him
You are His special guest.

Feel not that you are alone in this world
For there is someone praying for you
Feel not that you must carry your burdens alone
For there is someone who will carry you through.

Know that the Lord is with you always
He will never forsake you nor lead you astray
Enter into your prayer closet with gratitude
Give the Lord, your God, your request today.

Someone is giving thanks for you
Someone is remembering you in their prayers
Someone is asking God to give you wisdom
Someone is helping you with your cares.

Someone is crying in the darkest of night
that your wounded heart will be made whole
Enter into your prayer closet
Let your Lord and Saviour strengthened your soul.

Prayers are called up that God's love will heal you
Prayers are called up that God's word will keep you strong
Someone is praying that God will meet your every need
Enter into your prayer closet and truly see
That His great power is for us
who pray and believe.

"That he would grant you, according to the riches of his glory, to be strengthened with might by his Spirit in the inner man; That Christ may dwell in your hearts by faith; that ye, being rooted and grounded in love; May be able to comprehend with all saints what is the breadth, and length, and depth, and height; And to know the love of Christ, which passeth knowledge, that ye might be filled with all the fulness of God."
Ephesians 3:16-19

A Prayer For Strength

As I make my way towards the road called recovery
I must travel even when I am tired and worn
When I started my journey, I was so lost and confused
I needed to know which way to turn.

This illness has sapped all of my energy
I am ready to give up, my body is spent
I must bow down right now and begin to pray
I need for the Lord to bless me with strength.

Oh heavenly, most gracious God
You are Almighty and you are Omnipotent
You are the doctor in the time of trouble
Please provide me with your perfect strength.

My body, my mind shows signs of the battle
That has caused much pain for too long
I am weary… I need you Lord to heal me
Before my last breathe is surely gone.

I want to give you the honor and the glory
For I know you will guide me on the right path
That will provide the spirit of healing
With you Lord, I know this illness will pass.

I pray for your comforting angels
To camp about me every day and night
For there are times when I am weak and so alone
Knowing you are there will make everything all right.

My Lord, I ask for your grace, which is sufficient
May your power rest upon me I pray
In my weakness, your strength will be made perfect
Thank you for loving me and caring this way.

I humbly bow before you wounded and afflicted
I am here to do your Holy Will
I will have the faith of a tiny mustard seed
To believe that with Jesus stripes I am healed.

Most merciful God, thank you for being my strong tower
Lord, I will wait on you for I now can proclaim
Because of your undying love I can conquer all
Thank you for making me victorious, in Jesus name.
Amen.

"The Lord is my strength and my shield; my heart trusted in him,
and I am helped: therefore my heart greatly rejoiceth; and with my
song will I praise him."
Psalm 28:7

Healing Presence

Dear Lord, when I feel so all alone
I just want to be near your throne
Because you give to me the peace I need.
Oh Lord, when I am weak and in such pain
I just call upon your Holy name
Right then I feel your strength within me.

Lord, when my friends are nowhere to be found
And everything is turning upside down
I need your saving grace and mercy.
Oh Lord, when I fall down on my knees
With tears I cry please, Lord please
Come down right now and heal me.

Lord, I cannot make it own my own
I need you with me to go on
This illness has gone on for far too long.
So Lord, when I am in despair
I know you will answer all my prayers
Show me your love and make me strong.
Holy Spirit, descend upon me I pray
Rain down your mighty power today
Shower me with your everlasting love
Lord, wash away all my iniquities
Cleanse me, remove all the pain within me
Forgive me for the wrong that I have done.
Oh Lord, cure me so I will be made whole
Heal me Lord to save my soul
For this earthly vessel can't take the strain no more
So Lord, as I bow before your throne
May your healing presence touch me with a song
That will praise you for evermore.

Your healing presence I praise you for
Your everlasting peace I will adore
Your love, your grace and mercy have healed me.
Your power, your might, your joy, your rain
Your healing presence has erased the pain
And now my heart has a song to sing
Lord, thanks for healing me
thanks for saving me, thank you for loving me
In Jesus name,
Amen.

"Heal me Oh Lord, and I will be healed. Save me, Oh Lord, and I will be saved. For you are worthy to be praised."
Jeremiah 17:14

Comfort Me

As I lift my eyes up to the sky
I behold such a wondrous sight
Of beautiful clouds and a rainbow
Arching over a flock of geese in flight.

How high the mountains stretch upward
How vast the pastures roll
How bright the sunlight that pours down upon me
How magnificent God's creation unfolds.

When I think of all the goodness
When I think of all the joy
When I think of all the battles won
I thank God for saving my soul.

For I know He has shown favor to me
When I was sick and all alone
I know He placed his arms around me
When I was weak and feeling scorned.

I know that He has comfort me
When death knocked at my door
I know that He has sustained me
When I knew I could not make it anymore.

God created the tiny sparrows
And all other creatures, great and small
But when He created man and his woman
He showed us He loved us most of all.

By having His only son, Jesus
Die on the cross at Calvary
To pay for our sins and rise again
I knew in his heart He had a place for me.

So as I lift my eyes up to the sky
It is heaven that I am looking for
Until time is no more, my Lord will comfort me
To God be the glory
now and forevermore.

Praise Report

Whose report will you believe?
Is it the report of the Lord or the enemy?
When the storms of life are hopelessly raging
Do you praise the Lord or are you just complaining?

Do you gain patience through every trial?
Do you hold fast when the rain falls from the clouds?
Do you praise the Lord when times are tough?
Or do you just plain give up?

When your body is aching, whom do you turn to?
When your heart is breaking, who will see you through?
When your soul needed deliverance; who paid the price?
It was your Lord and Savior, Jesus Christ.

Praise the Lord from whom all blessings flow
Praise the Lord for the grace and mercy He shows
Praise him for bringing you through the pain
Praise him for the shelter from the rain.

So lift up your hands and give glory to the King
Sing praises for He has blessed you tremendously
Magnify Him for his love will last forevermore
Trust Him and always give
a praise report of the Lord.

"Make a joyful noise unto God, all ye lands: Sing forth the honour of
his name: make his praise glorious."

Psalm 66:1-2

"That the trial of your faith, being much more precious than of gold that perisheth, though it be tried by fire, might be found unto praise and honour and glory at the appearing of Jesus Christ."

1 Peter 1:7

Sorrow

Psalm 13:1-3

[1]How long wilt thou forget me, O LORD? for ever? how long wilt thou hide thy face from me? [2]How long shall I take counsel in my soul, having sorrow in my heart daily? how long shall mine enemy be exalted over me? [3]Consider and hear me, O LORD my God: lighten mine eyes, lest I sleep the sleep of death;

The Rose Garden

A gardener must first chose a place to lay
His garden of flowers and seeds
Like the place we seek to talk to the Lord
A place of tranquility and peace.

Now plant the seeds into soil that is rich
Keep it clean—watch what you sow
Plant His word in your heart, keep Him first in your life
Trust in Him and you will behold.

The rose petals are soft; its fragrance is sweet
Enclosed tightly, its fresh scent bring calm
Like the love of God as He embraces you
Keeping you safe in his outstretched arms.

The stems carry water to nourish the rose
Like God's word and His spirit divine
Jesus is the way, the truth, and the light
He is the one true vine.

The thorns represent the sins of the world
They prick and hurt when they are touched
But once pruned and sheared and free from them
It is like being washed in His blood.

The rebirth of the rose when a new season begins
Is the result of great love and great care
Like God's promise of eternal life with Him
And knowing He will always be there.

Its leaves are an important part of the body
It absorbs light that helps life to refresh
Like the body of Christ that we give our life for
Once we believe, and once we confess

That Jesus is Lord, He is our Saviour
He died on the cross for our sins
So that we can be included in the harvest to heaven
When God picks from His rose garden.

"And every one that hath forsaken houses, or brethren, or sisters, or father, or mother, or wife, or children, or lands, for my name's sake, shall receive an hundredfold, and shall inherit everlasting life. But many that are first shall be last; and the last shall be first."
Matthew 19:29-30

In God's Time

One Easter weekend a few years ago, my father suffered an aneurysm in the aorta of his heart. It blew his entire chamber into pieces and it shattered the lining of his chest. You would think that something like that would have killed him but the Lord knew at that moment it was not his time to go. So here is his story:

At the moment this was taking place, my father had told my mother that he did not feel well. He had just finished a piece of sweet potato pie (his favorite) and thought he was having indigestion. However, as the night moved on, he began to realize that maybe this was a very serious situation. He had watched a television show only the day before that informed him about taking an aspirin if you think you are having a heart attack. Therefore, he figured he had better take an aspirin for the pain. My parents had been married for 45 years by then. Some time ago, they had made a promise that if either one of them ever said they were "seeing stars", they would move fast to get themselves to the hospital. Around 1:30am, my father told my mother that he was seeing stars and my mother knew she had better get him to the hospital fast.

Since they only lived a few minutes from the general hospital, my father told her to drive him there. Before my mother could get dressed, my father had already put his coat on, walked out the front door, walked down the front steps, walked around the car, got in the car, started the car, got out of the car, walked back to the passenger side of the car and was waiting when my mother made it to the door. We are only talking a few minutes here. My mother said that she did not even remember driving to the hospital but when they got there, my father told her to park. He was not in a hurry. My father loved the Lord with all of his heart and he knew that the Lord would take care of him.

Once the doctors determined that this was a life-threatening situation, they had to rush him to the main hospital in another part of town for emergency surgery. The only thing that they could see on

175

the X-ray was a black screen…my father's blood had begun to travel off the highway onto the wide open road with no where to go. My mother did not want to go to the hospital alone so she called my oldest sister and told her to come and pick her up. My sister gave me a call and my family hit the road. It would take up to an hour to get there and it would become one of the longest days of our lives.

Before my father was wheeled into surgery, the doctor asked him if there anything that was worrying him. The doctor wanted him to be in the right state of mind before going in. My father told the doctor that the only thing worrying his mind was his wife. He told my mother right then that he loved her. The nurse almost started to cry because she thought that was the sweetest thing considering the danger that my father was in. My mother kissed my father goodbye but my father told her to not worry for he will be back. Little did he know that God was working a miracle right then and there.

The surgery took 7-8 hours during which time my other brothers and sister arrived. We had prayer sessions and crying sessions throughout the entire time. One special thing that my family did that others found hard to believe was that we consoled other families during their time of crisis also. We believed that no one should have to endure such heartache and pain alone so we helped others through prayer and scripture. When the doctor came out of surgery, he said that it was a miracle that my father was still alive. He could not believe the damage to his heart and because there was so much blood involved, they had to leave his chest open.

He said "Whatever you did while the surgery was being performed, it worked!" I told him that the only thing we did was put our trust in the Lord and believe that he will live through this.
This was Easter Sunday afternoon and I truly believed that if God could raise our Lord and Savior Jesus in three days then he could have mercy on my father and raise him too.

So for three days, his chest was left opened while his doctors figured out what the next course of action would be. There had only been one other person to live through this and that person died after 2 days. They knew that the Lord protected my father. My father actually died many times that week and was brought back to life. He remained in recovery for a month because they could not move him for fear it would kill him. He was unconscious for that period but we knew that he could hear us. We prayed over him, sang hymns to him, and read to him. We did not allow any negative words or thoughts be allowed in his room. He was only surrounded with all of the love that we had for him.

After many months, five to be exact, my father got to come home. He told me that while he was "away", he had a talk with the Lord. He asked him for time to take care of his home and his family. And the Lord blessed him with his request. The Lord gave my father three more years on this earth and during that time he praised the Lord in song and with deeds. And although he was in tremendous pain, he still continued to live his life for his family and for the Lord. My father died on May 19, 2000, in my mother's arms. He had fought a hard battle during those last three years of his life but we thank the Lord everyday for giving him back to us for that short time. And although we miss him terribly, his struggle was our life lesson to trust in the Lord and to love one another always.

God will answer prayer and God will deliver. But you must believe in Him to receive his blessings. Your help will come from the Lord and He will always come through in time. Give your life to the Lord and be prepared for a miracle in your life.

*"I will lift up mine eyes unto the hills, from whence cometh my help.
My help cometh from the LORD, which made heaven and earth.
He will not suffer thy foot to be moved: he that keepeth thee will not slumber.
Behold, he that keepeth Israel shall neither slumber nor sleep.
The LORD is thy keeper: the LORD is thy shade upon thy right hand.
The sun shall not smite thee by day, nor the moon by night.
The LORD shall preserve thee from all evil: he shall preserve thy soul.
The LORD shall preserve thy going out and thy coming in from this time forth,
and even for evermore."
Psalm 121*

A Time To Prepare

Dedicated In Loving Memory Of
My Father
Charles Milton Robinson, Sr.
1930-2000

My father went to heaven one day in May
He watches over me from up there
But before he made his last journey
He asked the Lord for time to prepare.
For three years before he left this place
He was hit with a mighty blow
For weeks his life hung in the balance
If he would make it, we did not know.

He had a special talk with the Lord
During that time of tremendous suspense
To ask Him to spare his life this time
To take care of some unfinished business.
He said, "Lord, I know I have not done all that I can
To make sure my family is cared for"
He said, "Lord, just give me some time to prepare them
For what you have in store".

"I must take time to tell them I love them
I must take time to get things arranged
I must take time to organize my finances
I must take time despite all my pain".
"For I know my journey will end soon
It saddens me that I will have to go
So Lord, I need time to tell them
That it is you they must depend on".

So for three years my father toiled
Despite pain, affliction, and hurt
He gave God the glory and honor

179

For his time let here on earth.
He told his wife that he loved her
Told his children to be what God expects
He took care of his home and his finances
He showered his family with love and respect.

When his time had finally arrived
All of his suffering had now ceased
He boarded his chariot to heaven
And he thanked the Lord for giving him peace.

In my mother's arm my father had died
For his time had come to an end
"Live your life for the Lord and be prepared" he said.
So we can see him in heaven again.

Celebrate My Life

Celebrate my life and let it be
A reminder of God's love and His glory
For I have lived my life fully for the Lord
Where my home is now there will be pain no more.

Tears that are shed should be of great joy
For I am now free from this old sinful world.
I have ascended into heaven
I will never be the same
For I have gone to glory where the angels reign.

Take from my life the wisdom to grow
Take from my life the knowledge to show
To others the love of our Saviour Divine
For He has truly blessed this old life of mine.

Sorrow may come in the still of the night
In your heart you may grieve and that is all right
But rejoice when the Lord shows you a brand new day
And cry no more, I am with the Lord for always.

Celebrate my life and let it be
A reminder to live your life completely
Praise the Lord for all blessings and live by His holy ways
So I may see my family in heaven again someday.

"And all thy children shall be taught of the Lord; and great shall be
the peace of thy children."
Isaiah 54:13

"Who can find a virtuous woman? For her price is far above rubies."
Proverbs 31:10

Called To Glory

My brother, you were called to do a marvelous work
While you were here on this great earth
You were a shining light for all to see
But the day came and you were called to glory.

You were called because God had a plan
To use your life as an example for man
It showed that being loving, honest, kind, and true
Will bring rewards from heaven to reign down upon you.

Know that you did not live your life in vain
For to your family God has made it very plain
That if we give our hearts, our lives to the Lord
We will be called to glory and will see you once more.

Rejoice when the day shall come
When we are all together in our heavenly home
Keep a watchful eye upon us we pray
Dear brother, we will see you again someday.

"But if the Spirit of him that raised up Jesus from the dead dwell in
you, he that raised up Christ from the dead shall also quicken your
mortal bodies by his Spirit that dwelleth
in you."
Romans 8:11

Heaven's Door

Dedicated In Loving Memory Of My Brother
Anthony C. Robinson
1958 — 1986

Dear brother, when will we meet again
    Since your life has now come to an end?
He answered — We will meet one day at heaven's door
    Since we both truly love our Saviour, our Lord.

Dear brother, when will my joy return?
    You are no longer with me; oh my heart does hurt.
He answered — Your sorrow may be dark as the night
    But the Lord promised joy with the morning light.

Dear brother, why did you have to leave?
    When you know this pain will consume all of me.
He answered — When you feel such grief and despair
    Give the Lord your burdens; He will hear your prayers.

Dear brother, do you see these tears in my eyes?
    To not be able to kiss you, to hug you just makes me cry.
He answered — Where I am I have been set free
    Rejoice and be glad! Cry no more for me.

Dear brother, did you know that I loved you so?
    I will miss you my dear brother more than you will know.
He answered — Just live your life fully for the Lord
    And I will meet you one day at heaven's door.

"Blessed are they that do his commandments, that they may have
right to the tree of life, and may enter in through the gates of the
city."

Revelations 22:14

"Blessed are they that mourn; for they shall be comforted."
Matthew 5:4

The Healing Prayer

As I walk along this road full of hurt and pain
I feel so alone: I cannot bear the strain
I know that my help come from thee, Oh Lord
But I am so weak and I cannot take it any more.

I talked to my best friend and she told me to be strong
And reminded me that I will not bear these burdens alone
She let me know that I can count on her to be there
Then she told me to fall on my knees and together we said this
prayer:

Dear Lord, as I struggle with the lost of my dear love one
I know that you were there when his life had begun
The void that I feel is now filled with your love
For I truly know that he is with you in heaven above.

I miss my father so dearly; the pain is so hard to bear
Oh Lord, give me the strength; let me know that you are near
Lord, I ask that you lift the burdens and lighten the weight
For the memories are unbearable, it is more than I can take.

I ask for your love to surround me, please hold me in your arms
I ask that you give me the courage to face this without harm
I ask that you give me peace to help me understand
And I thank you so much for including him in your glorious plan.

I thank you for the blessings you bestowed upon us all
I thank you for each day you gave us to stand tall
I thank you for my life for it is a story untold
Your love wrote each wonderful chapter; a love to behold.

As I bow down before you, Lord hear my plea
I ask for your divine spirit to indwell within me
I ask that you release me from this misery and gloom
I ask that you cleanse my heart and make your presence known.

I give my life to you Lord and I will give you all the praise
For all of the dark clouds that may come my way
I thank you Lord for my family and for saving my soul
And for giving me a friend to let me know that...
My help comes from the Lord.

I give you all the honor, I give you all the glory
I give you the praise for my love one's life story
Because you are God omnipotent I know I can live again
In Jesus name, I am healed. Hallelujah! Amen.

"He heals the brokenhearted and binds up their wounds."
Psalm 147:3

An Angel Called Alice

An Angel has ascended into heaven above
This world will not be same without her love.

She touched our lives with her sweet, sweet smile
Her hugs, her kisses made you feel worthwhile.

She was truly a wonderful friend to have
One that was always caring,
she made friendships that last.

She was respected and admired
She was noble and trusting
She was honest and devoted
She was kind and forgiving.

She would gather you into her loving arms
And make you feel happy with her charm.

She was a beautiful person
So God chose her today
Because she loved Him dearly in every way.

The angel that ascended into heaven now rest
She watches over us and we are blessed.

Her name is Alice
She is now with the Lord
And she will live in our hearts
Forevermore.

"Whatever is true, whatever is noble, whatever is right, whatever is
pure, whatever is lovely, whatever is admirable — if anything is
excellent or praiseworthy — think about such things."
Philippians 4:8

Our Guiding Light

In Loving Memory of
Christine Celest Hinton
1992-2001

She was here today full of life and love
    her light now shines brighter than the stars.
We thought it would be an ordinary night
    knowing we would see her with the rise of the sun.

Even though we know tomorrow is not promised,
    the Lord just may bless us with another day.
So our thoughts never wondered
    if she would leave us before her time.

Seeing her laugh and play
    thinking nothing could go wrong...
We did not know our last moments with her
    were now upon us...
        for she lived her life fully to the end.

Her marvelous light now shines bright
    as the morning star in heaven.
It guides us through this time
    of pain and sorrow.

And even though tears may flow
    during the darkest of night...
Joy comes in the morning
    because her light brings hope,
        it brings peace,
        it removes the darkness.

She now guides us with her love…
her wonderful memories bring smiles to our faces.
Like the lighthouse brings hope
to a ship on a tossed and driven sea,

She bring rays of happiness to our souls,
beams of peace to our heart,
and she lights the path to heaven.

Because of her love she will always be……
our guiding light.

"But the path of the just is as the shining light, that shineth more and
more unto the perfect day."
Proverbs 4:18

The Widow's Prayer

As I lay my head down for a long night's rest
I am filled with sweet sorrow, I can not survive another test
For the strain has been too hard for me to bear
Dear Lord I ask you to please hear my prayer...

Oh, most gracious Father, my Saviour, my rock
As I bow down before you on bended knees
I bring to you such a heavy heart
It is shattered into many pieces you see.

The void that was left by my dear husband
When he boarded his chariot home
Is like a never-ending darkness
That is filled with the melody of a widow's song.

I miss him so much Lord, it hurts so deep
This pain just cuts like a sharp knife
How can I carry on without him
For he was my all in all, he was my whole life.

I cry out to you Lord for only you know
This burden that is pressing me down
Into a deep, dark abyss of unhappiness
Oh Lord, please rescue me now.

The tears that run down my cheeks
Cannot wash away this agony I feel
Oh Lord, my God, please save me
For I just want to die and be with him.

But as I remember my family
I know I can not leave here just yet
For their pain is as real as mine
Lift their spirits and fill them with your Holiness.

190

So Lord, I pray for your comfort to sustain me
During this difficult time in my life
I pray for tranquility and sweet relief
Help me to overcome this misery and strife.

I pray for your strength when I am weak
I pray for the guidance of your loving hand
I pray for your mercy and your grace
I thank you for blessing me with a wonderful man.

Praise be to you Lord, Oh God
I lift my hands in reverence to you today
In you, Oh Lord, I found my strong refuge
To be able to survive the oncoming days.

So I thank you dear Lord for all of the years
You have given to me with my loving husband
You are my rock and my salvation
I long to be with him soon once again.

So do not let the floodwaters of grief engulf me
Answer me Lord out of the goodness of your love
Redeem me from my pain and my distress
Rain down your Spirit upon me from heaven above.

Praise be to your glorious name
Thank you Lord for your marvelous deeds
May the earth be filled with your glory
In Jesus name, thank you Lord for comforting me.

And the prayer of faith shall save the sick, and the Lord shall raise
him up; and if he has committed sins, they shall be forgiven him.
Confess your faults one to another, and pray one for another, that ye
may be healed. The effectual fervent prayer of a righteous man
availeth much."
James 5:15 — 16

Sorrow, oh sweet sorrow
Tears of sorrow fall in the dark of night
But joy, oh amazing joy comes
with the dawning of the morning light.

"And it shall come to pass in the day that the LORD shall give thee
rest from thy sorrow, and from thy fear, and from the hard bondage
wherein thou wast made to serve."
Isaiah 14:3

"Who is among you that feareth the LORD, that obeyeth the voice of
his servant, that walketh in darkness, and hath no light? let him trust
in the name of the LORD, and stay upon his God. Behold, all ye that
kindle a fire, that compass yourselves about with sparks: walk in the
light of your fire, and in the sparks that ye have kindled. This shall
ye have of mine hand; ye shall lie down in sorrow."
Isaiah 50:10-11

Remembering Thomas
Dedicated In Loving Memory of Thomas E. Warren
1954 — 1997

He gave his whole life unselfishly to the Lord
All of his days he praised his holy name
His reward was a passage to heaven
Here on earth, life without him is not the same.

He was filled with the Holy Spirit
He was kind hearted to all he would meet
You could take one look at him and know
That it was the Lord's grace he would diligently seek.

He knew that if the Lord was made first
Then his family would always be cared for
Just in case the Lord had a change in plans
To have his chariot come early for him to board.

His love for his wife was everlasting
His love for his children was so great
He showed them how to care for one another
Because he had a unexpected journey to make.

He taught them to rely on God's Word
He taught them to have courage and to be strong
He taught them to never give up or give in
Because the Lord has blessed them since they were born.

He was a wonderful friend and mentor
He was a man of honor and integrity
He was faithful and obedient even during his pain
Because it was the Lord in whom he believed.

When his struggles with cancer became evident
When he could not carry this burden anymore
The Lord said "Here is my faithful servant"
And then lifted him up on his chariot for home.

The Lord said, "I will reward you the passage to Heaven
For you have loved Me with all of your heart
Your family will be blessed for all times"
And he responded, "How great Thou art!".

"You have showed them how to love me
You will see them once again
Through your death, they will learn how to persevere
And to be strong against the evils of sin".

So he left his family in the hands of the Lord
He now watches over them and they miss him so much
Thank you Lord for blessing us with his undying love
Tears of joy now flow remembering Thomas.

"His lord said unto him, Well done thou good and faithful servant:
thou hast been faithful over a few things, I will make thee ruler over
many things: enter thou into the joy of thy Lord."
Matthew 25:21

Leave Love Behind

Although I am no longer with you
Do not cry for me today
Give your tears to someone who is hurting
Give them hope for a brighter day.
As you look upon this earthly vessel
What you see is only a shell
That housed the soul of God's own child
I thank the Lord for His love and care.

I pray that I lived my life
As an example of unwavering faith
For I knew that I had a Savior
Who loved me with so much mercy and grace.
I can leave behind my problems
But they would only bring you pain
I can leave behind my sorrows
But you would only cry tears like rain.

I can leave behind my possessions
But they would eventually fade away
I can leave behind my yesterdays
But they will not do anything for you today.
I can only leave you peace
In knowing that I am heaven bound
I can only leave you hope
In knowing that my God is always around.

I can only leave you joy
For in the morning things will seem brighter
I can only leave you happiness
For with God your burdens will be lighter.
And lastly I will leave you love
For it was love that saved my soul
When Jesus died for me at Calvary
He loved me so much that now I am whole.

I leave you love for it is the only thing that will last
Only love in knowing that my suffering has past
Jesus is seated at the right hand of God
At His feet is where I will be
So do not grieve for me
but rejoice
For I now rest in perfect peace.

"Surely goodness and love will follow me all the days of my life, and
I will dwell in the house
of the LORD forever."
Psalm 23:6

When You Think Of Me

It may be hard to understand
All the burdens we must bear
All the crosses we must carry
All the tears we must shed.
But one thing is certain
Even in this time of pain and grief
That our gracious God will see you through
And He will bring you peace.

Don't look back at what might have been
My battle is now over; I am at rest
Though the trials of cancer has defeated this earthy body
My soul has withstood the test.
Though darkness may overwhelm you for a while
And sadness has pierced your heart
Rejoice in knowing I have no regrets
For I know that all is not lost.
For you see when you think of me
Think about giving your life to the Lord
Do not put it off another day
For that day just may not come.
When you think of me
Think about how you treat one another
When you think of me
Think about how you are dearly loved
When you think of me
Think about never giving up
When you think of me
Think of all the blessings
That God has given us.

Do not let the cares of this world
Keep you from making a lasting friend
Do not grieve too long for me
Rejoice for my pain has now come to an end.

Where I am, there will be no more dying
Where I am, there will be no more crying
Where I am, there will be no more pain
Where I am, there will be no more suffering.

So farewell for now, I'll miss you
Never to forget what your love meant to me
Someday we will meet again
Because in heaven, there is someone on whom you can depend
His name is Jesus Christ
He is your Savior, your friend
When you think of me dear love, think of Him.

"Blessed be the God and father of our Lord Jesus Christ, the Father of mercies and God of all comforts, who comforts us in all our tribulation, that we may be able to comfort those who are in any trouble, with the comfort with which we ourselves are comforted by God. For as the sufferings of Christ abound in us, so our consolation also abounds through Christ."
2 Corinthians 1:3-5

Stress

2 Corinthians 4:5-7

[5]For we preach not ourselves, but Christ Jesus the Lord; and ourselves your servants for Jesus' sake. [6]For God, who commanded the light to shine out of darkness, hath shined in our hearts, to give the light of the knowledge of the glory of God in the face of Jesus Christ. [7]But we have this treasure in earthen vessels, that the excellency of the power may be of God, and not of us.

God Will Lift You Higher

God will lift you up when your life is in turmoil.
He knows the troubles that consume you.
He is always there to catch you when you fall.
But the pain of constant tribulation is wearing you down.
Sometimes you wonder if He is there at all.

God will lift you higher.

You must humble yourself in the sight of the Lord
Be renewed in order to receive His help
In the storm He will provide inner peace
And when your joy turns into heaviness
Through the rain, He will bring you sweet relief.

God will lift you higher.

When anxiety drags you into a deep, dark abyss
When depression strikes your inner coil
To rise above, you must let him take hold
For He will lift you up from that dreadful place
Let Him have your burdens to lighten your load.

God will lift you higher.

When your self-esteem takes a spiral fall
When your body does not look like it should
Know that God loves you for who you are
Even when you do not love yourself
Always know that you are a child of the Lord.

God will lift you higher.

God will take care of you no matter the situation
Whether it is abuse, addictions, or lost love holding you down
When your heart is heavy and you have no one to turn to

God will lift you high on the wings of an eagle
His compassion and love will soar with you.

You are never alone.
God will lift you higher.

"I waited patiently for the LORD; and he inclined unto me, and
heard my cry.
He brought me up also out of a horrible pit, out of the miry clay, and
set my feet upon a rock, and established my goings."
Psalm 40:1-2

Press On

Over the horizon I see the dark clouds form
Fear and anxiety takes root in my soul
A storm of a very large magnitude
Is developing on the path that I must go.

I can go to the east where there are hills to climb
I can go to the west where valleys are deep
But God intended for me to go straight through
So this is the path that I must keep.

The closer I get towards the prize
Of the high calling of God
The harder the path that lays before me
It is like a twisting and winding road.

When the storms of life are raging
When the sea of problems grow large
When the iniquities of this world overpower you
You must hold on to the hand of God.

When trouble meets you face to face
When you are feeling weak, battered and torn
When you think that you can not take anymore
Do not give up, you must press on.

For your reward in heaven comes through the trials
Which works patience to stay on course
Which brings hope in the promise of eternal life
Because God's love will protect you when things get worse.

So press towards the mark, press through the storms
Press on even when you are filled with pain and strife
Speak only into your life God's Word which will strengthen you
For you can do all things through Jesus Christ.

"Consider it pure joy, my brothers, whenever you face trials of many kinds, because you know that the testing of your faith develops perseverance. Perseverance must finish its work so that you may be mature and compete, not lacking anything."
James 1:2-4

The Drama

Constant moments of chaotic proportions
emotional highs and sorrowful lows
swinging back and forth through a maze of destruction
the drama now unfolds.

Mesmerized by the pile of problems
money woes, relationships that are strained
hypnotized by the sympathetic listeners
so called friends on the phone that just rang.

Feeling hurt, lonely, and confused
cannot bear yet another disappointment
cry a river of tears and run up more bills
when shopping for clothes instead of paying the rent.

Looking for solace in food and drink
looking for love where there is no love given back
looking for answers to questions asked again and again
the drama continues on to the very next act.

A vicious cycle spins round and round
the drama writes yet another ugly chapter
if you want to break this chain of despair
then here is something you must go after.

Seek the Lord when things get out of hand
seek the Lord if you want this cycle to cease
He will bear your burdens and will sustain you
ask him to bring you sweet relief.

Know that your friends cannot provide the answers
know that you will not find it in money or fame
know that only the Lord can bless you
with the Lord, no more drama, no more pain.

"And God shall wipe away all tears from their eyes; and there shall be no more death, neither sorrow, nor crying, neither shall there be any more pain: for the former things are passed away."
Revelation 21:4

Help In The Time of Trouble

Dear God,

The days have been ablaze under the heat of the sun
My mind wanders aimlessly for I am weak and so worn
My heart pounds with fury; my strength has failed
Crushed by the pains of this life my health is not well...

God,
I need your help.

I cannot see the blessings that I have received from you
The valleys are filled with hopelessness and distress
Overwhelmed by each trial, I am tired, I must rest...

God,
I need your strength.
There is a mountain of problems blocking my view

I will refrain from anger, I will turn from wrath
For these situations I know will not always last
I will walk with the Holy Spirit when times get tough
I will stay strong in the Word; I will not give up...

God,
I need your peace.

My tearful eyes will look beyond the hills
Beyond the valleys which stress has filled
I will look only to Thee for my help comes from you
I will wait patiently; it is what I must do.

God,
I need your grace.

No promise of an easy road so onward I must travel
For in times of trouble, the path of life will unravel
But to find my way I must search my aching heart
To persevere through the trials, I must press towards the mark
And praise his holy name; O' Lord, how great Thou art
For He restored my soul with a love that will never depart.

And God's answer.
I need you too.

"Let us not become weary in doing good, for at the proper time we
will reap a harvest if we do not give up"
Galatians 6:9

Call To Duty For the Most High

Your mind is a battlefield
And the devil knows it
He lies in the trenches
Waiting to attack you
If your troops are not ready
Which are your thoughts
If your platoon is not equipped
Which is your body
If your commander is not ready
Which is your spirit
Then get ready for the fight of your life
Because the enemy is always seeking
That place of weakness that lies in your mind
He is looking to devour you
And he know just where to start
He uses your past to weaken you
He uses family and friends to cut you down
He will use anything that will take your energy
He will use everything to take your focus from God
Therefore, you must put on your armour
You must be prepared
To do battle for the Lord; you must be aware
You must be strong to protect your heart
In order to dodge the devil's fiery darts
You must instill God's Word deep within you
You must be ready to be call to spiritual duty
In order to stand against the devil's plan of attack
Put on truth and righteousness for protection
Grab your bible, the Word, which is your sword
Draw into your soul the peace of God
Protect your mind with the helmet of salvation
And be filled with the Holy Spirit to survive
Guard yourself with love; always have your shield of faith
Be diligent to stand on God's promises which is your firm foundation
Keep your thoughts on the Word; pray without ceasing

Keep your eyes on God; it is his face you are seeking
No matter the pain or the price or the warfare in your life
Know that nothing is impossible for God
You will be the victor and the devil will be defeated
He will lick his wounds and go away for a season
He will lie in the trenches until another opportunity presents itself
For he wants to consume you
Fear not; be strong, for with God nothing can go wrong
Be always prepared and always pray to start your day
So that in every battle you are victorious
You are called to duty for the Most High
And you will never fight alone.

"Wherefore take unto you the whole amour of God, that ye may be
able to withstand in the evil day, and having done all, to stand."
Ephesians 6:13

God's Love is Beautiful

Bright sunny day
No clouds in the sky
Sweet gentle breeze
Flowers blooming all around
Hear the sound of laughter
Children on the playground
As far as the eye can see
God's love is beautiful.

Problems just vanish
Broken ties are on the mend
Relationships are strengthened
Another trial has disappeared
Survived another battle
Just won another race
As happy as the heart can feel
God's love is beautiful.

His love never changes
Will never leave you astray
Never, ever dying
God's love will last always
He will never forsake you
Your burdens He will bear
As wide as the arms can stretch
As high as the heavens rest
As deep as the deepest sea
As long as eternity
Look no farther than you and me
God's love is beautiful.

"Let your conversation be without covetousness; and be content with such things as ye have: for he hath said, I will never leave thee, nor forsake thee. So that we may boldly say, The Lord is my helper, and I will not fear what man shall do unto me."
Hebrews 13:5-6

Temptation

James 1:12-13
[12] Blessed is the man who endures temptation; for when he has been approved, he will receive the crown of life which the Lord has promised to those who love Him.
[13]Let no one say when he is tempted, "I am tempted by God"; for God cannot be tempted by evil, nor does He Himself tempt anyone.

Prayer Does A Body Good

While gaining inches around my waist
I gained a new perspective
That my hips and thighs are getting wide
But it is a notion that I had rejected.

Denial is what it is called
Because I comfort myself with food
And I do not want to give it up
Because the stress just makes me blue.

I have tried every diet
I have tried every pill
I have tried everything that money can buy
But the battle goes on still.

What I found to be successful
In losing this burden that weighs me down
Is that I should give it to the Lord
So I can start losing some of these pounds.

I tried to do it on my own
But I learned that in order to win
That I must keep my eyes on the prize
And have God not food as my friend.

So when the battle becomes too much
And my mind just dwells on food
I just ask the Lord for the strength to deny
Because prayer does a body good.

"…the LORD seeth not as man seeth; for man looketh on the
outward appearance, but the LORD looketh on the heart."
1st Samuel 16:7

"Blessed is the man that endureth temptation: for when he is tried, he shall receive the crown of life, which the Lord hath promised to them that love him. Let no man say when he is tempted, I am tempted of God: for God cannot be tempted with evil, neither tempteth he any man: But every man is tempted, when he is drawn away of his own lust, and enticed. Then when lust hath conceived, it bringeth forth sin: and sin, when it is finished, bringeth forth death. Do not err, my beloved brethren."

James 1:12-16

Tempted By Desire

One look at you and my heart thus melts
into a sea of flowing desire
Every minute, every second I am near you
Your presence burns deep with its fire.

This feeling is full of passion
This feeling is powerful, so very strong
This feeling is quite overwhelming
This feeling is so very wrong.

Temptation has wrapped its arms around me
It is leading me into a dangerous place
Although this feeling is soothing to the mind
It will only lead us to heartache.

You are my friend to whom I can turn to
You are a person who I do adore
I am weak when I am around you
Which is why I cannot see you anymore.

When you touch me it sends me spinning
When you look at me it makes me cry
For I can see you care very deep for me
But you have a family and so do I.

I could let temptation take me by the hand
And lead me onto the path of desire
But instead I must ask God for forgiveness
And repent for being weak this very hour.

I will ask that He forgive you too
For there is a cost for one brief moment of sin
It is paid through the pain that secrets will bring
It will cost us everything including heaven.

Temptation will come again to rob us
And our passion for life will again overflow
Which is why the desires of our hearts must be on Him
For God love us more than we will ever know.

"For all that is in the world, the lust of the flesh, and the lust of the
eyes, and the pride of life, is not of the Father, but is of the world.
And the world passeth away, and the lust thereof: but he that doeth
the will of God abideth for ever."
1st John 2:16-17

A Thursday To Remember

As the feast draws nigh
As the sun begins to set
A crime of the heart was taking place
When a disciple failed his test.
Tempted by the enemy's money
To Satan he sold his soul
Iscariot was his surname
A deadly promise for a bag of gold.

The plot was now laid
To betray the one he claimed to love
Conspiring to turn in the Lord Jesus
A life for a bag of gold.
As preparation were being made
For the Passover, the last supper
The prophecy was now coming to past
That our Lord and Savoir would suffer.
This is my blood that was shed for you
Do this in remembrance of me
This is my body that was given to you
Do this in remembrance of me.
After breaking of bread and lifting of cup
Jesus said "My betrayal is now at hand
For at this very table
Is seated the one, much woe unto this man".

It is a pity that not just one but many
Disciples would think that it was them
But one named Judas knew the truth
That only he could betray such a friend.
After the Lord's Supper they went to Mount Olive
Where Jesus told them to pray for strength
To not enter into temptation
But instead they all just slept.
Then behold came a multitude

With a kiss Jesus fate was sealed
At that point the prophecy was completed
For the next day Jesus was killed.
Three days later Jesus would rise again
Dying for our sins and saving our souls
But it is Thursday that Judas will remember
When he sold his life for a bag of gold.

"And when they had bound Him, they led Him away and delivered Him to Pontius Pilate the governor. Then Judas, His betrayer, seeing that He had been condemned, was remorseful and brought back the thirty pieces of silver to the chief priests and elders, saying, "I have sinned by betraying innocent blood." And they said, "What is that to us? You see to it!" Then he threw down the pieces of silver in the temple and departed, and went and hanged himself."
Matthew 27:2-5

Unforgiveness

Psalm 97:10-12
[10] Let those who love the LORD hate evil,
for he guards the lives of his faithful ones
and delivers them from the hand of the wicked.
[11] Light is shed upon the righteous
and joy on the upright in heart.
[12] Rejoice in the LORD, you who are righteous,
and praise his holy name.

The Power Of Forgiveness

Do I waste precious time
carrying around this hurt and pain?
Do I waste precious energy
dragging around this guilt and shame?
Can I move beyond the heartache
and begin to mend again?
Only the power of forgiveness
can heal my broken heart within.

Unfinished business
Unresolved issues
Unwilling to change
Unwilling to move
Are a few of the many reasons
Why people hold a grudge or two.

Holding on to the hurt
Holding on to the pain
Holding on to the anger
Holding on to the past
Only keeps you held hostage
To the chains of resentment
Allowing hatred to fester and last.

God's powerful Word says
you must forgive your brother
Just as Jesus had forgiven you
God's mighty Word says
you must let go of the past and move forward
Replace the anger with love
is what you must do.

Forgiveness
is not only for the other person
who may have allowed
this pain to ruin your life
But it is for you personally
to always remember
the power of forgiveness
begins with
Jesus Christ.

"Therefore I say unto you, What things soever ye desire, when ye pray, believe that ye receive them, and ye shall have them. And when ye stand praying, forgive, if ye have ought against any: that your Father also which is in heaven may forgive you your trespasses. But if ye do not forgive, neither will your Father which is in heaven forgive your trespasses."
Mark 11:24-26

Affirmations

You must vision yourself as a child of God
Royalty and blessed, cherished and love
Believe in yourself; remove all negative thoughts
As you repeat each of these to yourself in the mirror.

I am a child of God
I am a royal priesthood
I am loved, I am blessed
I am beautiful
I am creative
I am a true survivor
I can withstand any test
I am a woman of God
I am a person of honor
I am talented
I am forgiven
I am full of joy
I am at peace
I am strong
I am definitely courageous
I am a good mother
I am a good father
I am a very good husband
I am a very good wife
I am a hard worker
I am a caring person
I am a great friend
I will rise above strife
I will not accept defeat
For I am victorious
I will not accept lies
For I am filled with God's truth
I will not accept what the world wants to give me
For I have a heart that has been renewed.
All I have to do each and everyday

Is have faith and believe
I have a Saviour named
Jesus Christ
With Jesus, I am redeemed
With Jesus, I am saved by grace
With Jesus, I am restored
I will say these affirmations every day
To remind myself
I belong to the Lord.

"Give ear to my words, O LORD, consider my meditation. Hearken unto the voice of my cry, my King, and my God: for unto thee will I pray. My voice shalt thou hear in the morning, O LORD; in the morning will I direct my prayer unto thee, and will look up."
Psalm 5:1-3

Sea of Forgiveness

Keeping an account of all the wrongs
that you had suffered through
Letting the feelings of resentfulness
just steadily rise up within you
Allowing the pain, the shame, and the guilt
to bring more misery and strife
It is what happens when unforgiveness
takes over your entire life.

The devil likes to throw up the old photos
and bring to remembrance the hurtful times
When your friends, your spouse, your family
or even your coworkers may have lied.

He likes to remind you of all of the failures
you may had experienced during your life
Making sure you do not even forgive yourself
much less your child, your husband, your wife.

But God has a plan for those old photos
He will help you remove those fiery darts
It will take being obedient to follow his Word
For true forgiveness must come from the heart.

So toss into the sea of forgiveness
all the wrongs that are holding you down
Toss into the sea all misery, strife, and pain
Let the living waters of God cleanse you right now.

Let go of the guilt, let go of the grudge
Let it all be released so that you can be blessed
For the sins that once caused you anguish
Are now replaced by God's love and forgiveness.

"And be ye kind one to another, tenderhearted, forgiving one another, even as God for Christ's sake hath forgiven you."
Ephesians 4:32

Love Thy Neighbor As Thyself

When envy puts you to the test
Love thy neighbor as thyself
For material things can not bring happiness
Share what you have to be truly blessed.

When you see a person downtrodden
Remember they may only be forgotten
Let them know that the Lord does truly love them
Tell them to put their faith and trust in Him.

When a hungry person crosses your path
Give them food so their strength will last
For in every circumstance God keeps His promises
To those who are called to do deeds of kindness.

When you see a neighbor in need
Whether it is buying some groceries or raking the leaves
Help them during their trials and adversities
For the Lord shows favor to those living in unity.

When you do not truly love yourself
It is hard to show love to someone else
Know that God is love and He knows what is best
His commandment is simple:
Love thy neighbor as thyself.

"I have shewed you all things, how that so labouring ye ought to
support the weak, and to remember the words of the Lord Jesus, how
he said, It is more blessed to give than to receive."
Acts 20:35

Heavy Laden

Dear Lord, here I am before you again
With the weight on my shoulders feeling so heavy
For I bring to your Holy alter
The same bag full of pain, guilt, hurt, and worry.
I know if I just leave it here with you
I know I will feel a tremendous relief
But instead, I'll just try to carry it alone
After all, there is now a new burden, grief.

I must have carried this bag everyday of my life
For I rather have the pity of man
I continue to place in it mistakes and bitter tears
But I found this heaviness was not part of my plan.
Resentment, misery, anger, and strife
Decided to take a ride with me one day
I have let unforgiveness, pride, and low self esteem
Joined all the other burdens to my dismay.

So now here I am again dear Lord
For my bag is now too heavy to tote around
It is keeping me from moving forward in life
It is keeping me from being heaven bound.
I lay out to you, Lord, at the alter
This bag filled with every burden, need and care
I ask that you replace it with your perfect love
This is my request, this is my prayer.

Put in my bag the fruit of the spirit
Love, peace, and joy, meekness and faith
Put in longsuffering, temperance, and goodness
Fill it with gentleness, do whatever it will take.
I have not been obedient in seeing what matters
I ask for your forgiveness and your saving grace
For my load will be as light a feather
I can now go on and finish this race.

As I look into the future
I will not fret nor will I complain
For you said "Come unto me, all ye that labour ."
I have found rest in Jesus name.

"Come unto me, all ye that labour and are heavy laden, and I will give you rest."
Matthew 11:28

Unwilling To Change

Romans 12:1-3

[1]I beseech you therefore, brethren, by the mercies of God, that ye present your bodies a living sacrifice, holy, acceptable unto God, which is your reasonable service.

[2]And be not conformed to this world: but be ye transformed by the renewing of your mind, that ye may prove what is that good, and acceptable, and perfect, will of God.

[3]For I say, through the grace given unto me, to every man that is among you, not to think of himself more highly than he ought to think; but to think soberly, according as God hath dealt to every man the measure of faith.

Blocking My Blessings

Lately, I have been thinking about revitalizing my life. I have been feeling a little depressed. Yes, you heard me, *DEPRESSED*. My life seems to keep spinning in the same direction and running on the same path with no change in sight. Matter of fact, my life has been boring and mundane to me. So much so that I cannot imagine what my friends and family must be seeing. I have complained, dreamed, and even wished upon a star that I could get moving in another direction. But my "Self" keeps getting in the way. You see, I am comfortable for the most part with my life. I am thriving when it comes to my spiritual life although there is obviously much room for improvement. Who in their right mind would be depressed if their spiritual life was going great? I am doing alright with my job. But I am getting to the point of screaming that All-American chant of "Take this job and shove it!". I am just being brutally honest here. I think I have a good relationship with my children but life has told me that what you see may not be what's going on. I think I have a good relationship with my husband but the thrill has gone on down the road and I may have to ask Mr. B.B. King just where it went.

So in my frustration I shouted, "Self!". Now how many of you talk to yourself? Go ahead, raise your hand. As you can see, I do it all the time. I said, "Self, you have got to move out of the way! You are blocking my blessings." However, "Self" does not want to listen to me. I get a blank stare back every time when I looked in the mirror at my "Self". It was like the stare that I get when I tell my children to clean their rooms. "Are you talking to me?" is what my children would say and of course, I would let them know that I was really talking to the wall. "Self" responded in the same manner and it proceeded to ignore me. Now my children would know automatically that this kind of response was a "no-no" and would get them in hot water with dear old mom. But "Self" must have figured that since it was in control of my mind that it could act any way it wanted to. Feeling tired and defeated, I surrendered to "Self" and it just continue on with the same tired game plan day in and day out. My mind thought that if I just talk to "Will" (short for willpower) then maybe it could convince "Self" that a change has got to come. But good old willpower was just as tired as my body and mind. "Self" was getting on everybody's nerve and wearing all of us out. And it had reinforcements to help beat us down. It let "Negativity" and all of its relatives move in and take up residence. And that is why "Depression" is hanging out with me today.

Now I know how I can get rid of these old feelings. I know that all I have to do is pray and repent my slothful ways. But right now these feelings have got such a vice grip on my mind, body, and spirit that I am going to need help. I have tried doing this alone. Tried changing on my own. But "Motivation" is no where to be found. It has gone "M.I.A." as in missing in action. As I stated before, I am for the most part comfortable with my life. There are many things in my life that brings great joy to me. My work at the hospitals, my children and grand child, my continue growth in the bible, they all bring great joy to my life along with spending time with those that I love. But I have resented "Self" for a while now because it has become lazy in other areas. And because of its laziness, I am suffering.

You are probably wondering by now, "Is this Rose talking?" or is this a figment of your imagination. Your eyes and ears do not deceive you. It is definitely the lady that you all know as "Ms. Organization" and "Ms. Got A Smile On Her Face As Bright As Sunshine". Yes, I have to admit, it is all a front. My face does not show the wear and tear that "Self" has put upon my being. "Ms. Makeup" keeps the deception going. But on the inside, I am in trouble. The battle is continuous. My body keeps asking my mind, "How come I cannot lose this weight?" "Why is my hair so thin", "Why in the world are these pants fitting so tight when last week there was some room in the waist?" and so on and so on.

My body keeps asking my soul, "Where in the world is "Will" and "Motivation" at? And why isn't God answering your prayers?" Just like the hit song of the world singing "It's getting hot in here" so is my being which is on fire with a whole lot of confusion and finger pointing. Nothing was getting accomplished. Therefore, "Self", although pretty miserable, decided to continue to hang out with "Depression".

I guess it was easier to have a pity party than to get busy and make a change. So "Negativity", "Depression", "Stress" (you know them as the top dogs of the bunch) just partied on from dawn to dusk. Sometimes they even hung out after midnight just to see how many bags they can put on my face before the sun began to rise again. When I looked in the mirror I would say, "Self, you sure are looking rough this morning." and "Self "would say, "Then let me go back to bed." Of course, if it is a workday, my mind would give a reminder that I do need to get paid for there are bills that will be due. So I fight the thought and get ready to go to work. Of course, this may happen on Sunday when I am supposed to get up for church. But I have to admit that the spiritual part of me is much stronger and can resist that temptation. The yearning to want to know more about Jesus Christ is so strong that "Self" does not even bother asking to go back to bed anymore. But work, oh boy, now I could stay in the bed and let "Self" have all the sleep it wants. But something about bill collectors coming to visit do scare me therefore, I will get up and go to work.

I need to make a change. But it is apparent to me that I have to get busy moving towards that change. I can talk about doing it all I want to. And you should hear some of the conversations that I have in my mind. Change is good for your body. Change is good for your mind. And change is good for your soul. But you have to get moving. So today, I say to "Self", "It is time to move!". Once again, "Self" gives back a blank stare but this time I am ready for it. "I can do all things through Christ who strengthens me", I shouted back at the mirror. "Self" was beginning to believe it because I kept saying it over and over. But "Negativity", "Depression", and "Stress" all said, "You have been down this road before. We know that you will fail again. This weight is going to stay with you for the rest of your days. And there is nothing that you can do about it". I said, (with the zeal of the Nutty Professor) "Yes, I can! Yes, I can! Yes, I can! With God all things are possible for those who believe!" Well my "Self" started to feel a little stronger. Then I fell down on my knees in reverence to my Lord and begin to pray.

"Lord, break me from this bondage. I have failed miserably in the past when it came to making positive changes in my life. I ask that you help me to move my "Self "out of the way so I can give my life freely to you. I want to be a servant who does not have mountains of guilt and stress in the way. I want to be able to see my blessings that you bring to me. My eyes and my mind have been focused too long on the things of this world. I ask that you help me keep my eyes and my mind steadfast on you Lord. You are my God and I want to glorify you. I cannot do that if the temple that you reside in is full of junk. Help me to purge my heart, my soul, and my mind, in order for my spiritual being to flow free once again. I ask that you use me to the edification of your kingdom once the cleansing process is completed. My faith in you Lord is strong and I know a change is going to come. In Jesus name I pray. Amen."

With a sincere heart and a renewed mind, I was able to say "Self, move out of the way. It is time for a change so God can use me in a mighty way." My "Self" responded with a glorious thank you and praises to God for the strength because it was mighty tired also. It said, "Rose, it is about time! Just look up to the hills from whence cometh your help and call on the Lord. I would have told you this but you had to believe it. So now, just do it!" And with renewed love for myself, the great change begins.

"Set an example for the believers in speech, in life, in love, in faith, and in purity."
1 Timothy 4:12

Worry

Isaiah 42:16
[16] I will lead the blind by ways they have not known,
along unfamiliar paths I will guide them;
I will turn the darkness into light before them
and make the rough places smooth.
These are the things I will do;
I will not forsake them.

God, Are You There?

Hello God, it's me.
I mean, it is *(say your name)*
I called you yesterday about a situation
that I was dealing with.
I did not hear from you
Are you there?
Anyway, I just wanted to let you know
that the pain has not gone away.
My heart is still aching
and my whole body hurts.
Why have you not answered my prayer?
Hello, are you really there?
Maybe I have a bad connection
My prayer line does have a little static
and I have been distracted with other things
Matter of fact, I have to admit
that I did not even try contacting you
until things became too hard to bear
God, I just need to know if you are listening
I know I can thank you a whole lot better
if you would just take the pain away first
It is keeping my mind off of your Word
Your Word?
I know I should be looking at your Word
for guidance but I need to hear from you
Where are you?
Hello, can you hear me?
I know you may be busy with more pressing matters
like saving lives and stopping the enemy
But if you have just a little time
I need to give you this pain so
that I will feel much better.

"Hello, _(say your name)_. It is me, God."
Well, Praise the Lord, I can hear you!
"Then listen!" thus saith the Lord
"If you want to be healed
then turn your eyes to the hills
And there you will find me.
If you want to be saved
turn from your wicked ways
and there you will find peace.
If you want to be restored
then say "Create in me a clean heart, dear Lord"
And I will give you eternity."
After that, there was only silence
as I pondered on what God had said
I realized that God is never late
in answering my requests.

He is always right on time
I could only repent
because my faith had faltered
Realizing that all I had to do was just wait
patiently on the Lord
And believe in the One to which all things are possible
All I could do was say Thank you Lord
Thank you for loving me
Thank you for answering my prayers
I may not be able to see you Lord
but thank you for being there.

"Wait on the LORD; Be of good courage, And He shall strengthen
your heart; Wait, I say, on the LORD!"
Psalms 27:14

"I waited patiently for the LORD; and He inclined to me,
And heard my cry. He also brought me up out of a horrible pit,
Out of the miry clay, And set my feet upon a rock,
And established my steps. He has put a new song in my mouth —
Praise to our God; many will see it and fear,
And will trust in the LORD."
Psalms 40:1-3

"Behold, we count them happy which endure. Ye have heard of the
patience of Job, and have seen the end of the Lord; that the Lord is
very pitiful, and of tender mercy.
But above all things, my brethren, swear not, neither by heaven,
neither by the earth, neither by any other oath: but let your yea be
yea; and your nay, nay; lest ye fall into condemnation. Is any among
you afflicted? let him pray. Is any merry? let him sing psalms. Is
any sick among you? let him call for the elders of the church; and let
them pray over him, anointing him with oil in the name of the Lord:"
James 5:11-14

Imagine

Imagine a world without laws...
Would you even know right from wrong
If all laws were truly gone?
If you did not have authority to enforce them
Would you know which way to turn?
Would you accomplish very much or even care?
Or would you just sit there and be too scared
To move for fear that someone will do
Great harm to your family and you?
Now imagine a world without God...
Imagine no hope, no peace, no love
Imagine no sun, no light from above
Imagine only darkness, an earth without form
Imagine any of us not being born.
Imagine all the talents gone to waste
Imagine this world as a desolate place
Imagine the sadness, imagine the strife
That would happen because there is no life
Because the saddest part about this is
If God is not in your life, then you have no life to live.
Now imagine being buried 6 feet under in sin
Imagine the pressures of life consuming within
Laws can be broken and are a temporary fix
God is always able for He is omnipotent
To live in fear because you have no peace
To live in strife because your faith has ceased
You must imagine beyond this earthly realm
And know God has a better place called Heaven.
Now imagine pearly gates and streets made of gold
Imagine love that flows forevermore
Imagine peace and hope meeting you at the door
Imagine no more pain and crying no more
Imagine all the people who have gone before you
Imagine being reunited with those who were faithful and true
Imagine seeing your mother, father, sister, or brother

Imagine a happiness unlike no other.
Now imagine seeing Jesus at the right hand of God
A life without salvation is far worse than a world without laws
For with God all things are possible and He will never change
Laws will be broken and they will not remain
But one thing that is certain
No matter what the world may say
If it was not for the grace of God
We would not be here today
Now imagine that.

"For he has rescued us from the dominion of darkness and brought
us into the kingdom of the Son He loves, in whom we have
redemption, the forgiveness of sins."
Colossians 1:13-14

Faith, Hope, and Love

Faith, hope, and love came to visit me one day
But only the seed of faith decided to stay
It saw that my heart had an empty space
So it decided to move in and take its place
Once faith planted itself into my heart
My outlook on life grew bright from the start
For even though my faith was as small as a mustard seed
The light of God began to truly shine within me.

After faith came and took up residence
Hope decided it had some time to spend
So it came and visited my heart one day
And this was the message it had to say
"Your hope is built on nothing less,
Than Jesus' blood and righteousness,
If eternity in heaven is where you want to be
Then give your heart to Jesus and put your trust in Thee".

Hope and faith began to grow
Like bright morning stars they began to glow
The more prevalent they became in my life
The less there was in terms of pain and strife
Then love came and knocked on my heart's door
Faith and hope told it to enter for there was room for more
Once love entered the presence of God was made known
His Holy Spirit knew it was in the place where it belongs.

Filled with God's love my heart thus grew
And other wonderful attributes came to visit too
Joy, peace, and temperance came with meekness
Longsuffering and gentleness showed up with goodness
My heart overflowed with God's mercy and grace
Faith, hope, and love had filled my empty space
My heart was made strong by these blessings from above
But the greatest of these was love.

"And he said to the woman, Thy faith has saved thee: go in peace".
Luke 7:50

"Now our Lord Jesus Christ himself, and God, even our Father, which hath loved us, and hath given us everlasting consolation and good hope through grace. Comfort your hearts, and stablish you in every good word and work."
II Thessalonians 32:16-17

A Soldier's Price To Pay

Sometimes actions speak louder than word
So I am going to show you that my love is true
I will go into the lions den and stand firm
Even if it means dying for you.
For I know of someone who laid their life down for me
Someone I had not met but only heard about
But what I heard was that He died at Calvary
To save us all, this I have no doubt.

There are fathers and mothers, sisters and brothers
People all across this great land
Whom I have never met nor ever seen
But I chose to protect them the best way I can.
The many faces, names, and addresses
Of those who are depending on me
To stand firm, to be strong, to be diligent and brave
So that peace is ushered in with victory.

I can only imagine the great pain and strife
That my Lord must have suffered that day
When I look around at the destruction of life
I can only imagine the heavy price He had to pay.
For I understand the compassion that He must have felt
When they scorned Him and pierced his side
I can only imagine the love that He felt
As He gave up the ghost and died.

But Jesus rose again and salvation became mine
Which is why I must fight for the precious freedom
Of all people who are oppressed and buried alive
Under tyranny, dictatorship, and evil.
It is my humble prayer that God will protect me
It is my prayer that God will guide me through
It is my prayer that every woman and man in combat
Will come to know and love Jesus as I do.

So to my family, friends, and love ones
Whose faces I have seen all my life
I will have the courage and the strength to endure this ugly war
Because Jesus has already paid the price.

"Though an army besieges me, my heart will not fear;
though war breaks out against me, even then will I be confident.
One thing I ask of the LORD, this is what I seek: that I may dwell in
the house of the LORD
all the days of my life, to gaze upon the beauty of the LORD
and to seek him in his temple."
Psalm 27:3-4

In Tune With God

There is static in the air
Interference is all around me
As I raise my hand a little higher
It is getting harder to see clearly
As the fog of trouble comes rolling in
My vision becomes impaired
I start to slip, I start to stumble
Now distracted I am unaware
That my life is moving on the wrong path
I must stop it from going astray
But I cannot see nor even hear
The train that is coming my way
It is a wreak waiting to happen
As I cross blindly onto its tracks
A rush of wind suddenly surrounds me
Telling me to just turn back
Shall I go on? second guessing
The voice of reason that let me know
That if I keep going the way I am going
I am going to continue down a destructive road
Turn back! Turn back! The voice warned
Hold your hands up to the sky
Take a hold of someone who will guide you
Just do it, do not ask "Why?"
Move your hands to the left
And praise my Holy name
Move your hands to the right
Worship me for I will not change
Wave your hands in the air
Stretch your hands up towards the sky
Look up towards the hills for help
And take hold of the hand of God
For if I promised to always lift you
Out of the mire clay
Then have faith for I can surely lift you

High above the trouble that comes your way
Just like an antenna trying to get a reception
In order to receive help from above
You must praise and worship our Lord
You must remain focus on God's love
Whether you are sick or afflicted
Whether you are lonely or filled with despair
Lift up your eyes to the hills
And you will find help there
Lift up a song of thanksgiving
Lift up a heartfelt prayer of love
No matter what happens next
Stay in tune with God.

"I waited patiently for the LORD; and he inclined unto me, and heard my cry. He brought me up also out of an horrible pit, out of the miry clay, and set my feet upon a rock, and established my goings. And he hath put a new song in my mouth, even praise unto our God: many shall see it, and fear, and shall trust in the LORD."
Psalm 40:1-3

Prayer of Deliverance

Dear Heavenly Father
From whom the heavens and earth were formed
I give you the honor, the glory, and the praise
You are my Redeemer; you are my Lord.

Forgive me for my shortcomings
Help me to see the errors of my ways
For I know that I have let you down
When I keep turning away.

Lead me into a greater realm
of emotional health and security
Move on my behalf when I am discouraged
Turn my worries into peace.

Turn my sickness into healing
My fears into faith
Turn my despair into hope
Remove the guilt from my face.

Give me a greater portion of love
A greater portion of joy
A greater portion of faith
And all things hoped for.

You said in your Holy Word
whatsoever I shall ask in prayer and supplication
Believing, I shall receive blessings
beyond my wildest imagination.

I will stand on your promises dear Lord
But I know I have a part to do
That is to always give you honor and glory
And show the utmost reverence to you.

So deliver me Lord from my darkness
Into your marvelous light
Remove the shackles that have me bound
Please turn my miserable life around
My lips will forever praise thee
all day and all night.
In Jesus glorious name, I pray,
Amen.

"In thee, O LORD, do I put my trust; let me never be ashamed:
deliver me in thy righteousness. Bow down thine ear to me; deliver
me speedily: be thou my strong rock, for an house of defence to save
me. For thou art my rock and my fortress; therefore for thy name's
sake lead me, and guide me."
Psalm 31:1-3

About the Author

Rose Robinson Coleman lives in Parkersburg, WV, with her husband, 2 grown children, and grandson. She is a graduate of the historical black college, West Virginia State College, in Institute, West Virginia and a true believer of the Lord. She is inspired by the Holy Spirit to write according to God's Word. Through scripture verses, poetry, short essays, and prayer, Rose expresses the healing power and love that the Lord has for the broken hearted. She has spoken at many church services, retreats, and other local functions but her greatest opportunity to exhort the name of the Lord is through her church ministry called Angelic Outreach Ministry. It is an outreach ministry that touches those who are in the hospitals and nursing homes. This is her first book. May it bring glory and honor to the Lord.

Printed in the United States
21094LVS00006B/85-93